AN ANGLING MISCELLANY

AN ANGLING MISCELLANY

500 YEARS OF FISHING FIGURES, FACTS AND FANCIES

COMPILED BY TOM QUINN

Quiller

First published in the UK in 2026
by Quiller, an imprint of Amberley Publishing Ltd

British Library Cataloguing-in-Publication Data
A catalogue record for this book is available
from the British Library

ISBN 978-1-84689-437-4 (hardback)
ISBN 978-1-84689-438-1 (e-book)

Cover illustration by John Holder

Typesetting by SJmagic DESIGN SERVICES, India.
Printed in Great Britain

Quiller
An imprint of Amberley Publishing Ltd
The Hill, Merrywalks, Stroud, GL5 4EP
Tel: 01453 847800
Email: info@quillerbooks.com
Website: www.quillerpublishing.com

Appointed GPSR EU Representative: Easy Access System Europe Oü, 16879218
Address: Mustamäe tee 50, 10621, Tallinn, Estonia
Contact Details: gpsr.requests@easproject.com,
+358 40 500 3575

Contents

Introduction

HOW MANY rods and reels are manufactured each year; where is the oldest depiction of an angler in art; how many fish species are there; which is the world's most exclusive fishing club and what's the best-selling fishing book of all time? The answers to these and hundreds of other questions can be found in this most comprehensive angling miscellany.

Despite the popularity of football and other sports, angling remains the most popular participant sport in Britain and, when they are not fishing, Britain's one million-plus anglers can usually be found tucked up by the fireside and reading about their favourite pursuit. And what better book to accompany those fireside evenings than one that includes fishing's most fascinating facts and fancies – everything from the biggest fish ever caught on rod and line to the world's rarest fish, from a fish that can survive for years without water to a fish that draws pictures to attract a mate. And even a fish that lives for more than 500 years.

Also included are numerous unbelievable but true angling stories ancient and modern: the tale, for example, of the boy who caught a freshwater mussel containing forty pearls (they were sold for more than his father had earned in the previous five years); or the story of the boy who caught a record fish from a sewage outflow in north London; or the Victorian academic who insisted on trying to swim up a new salmon ladder just to make sure the salmon would be able to do it.

An Angling Miscellany is the ultimate collection for anyone who loves fishing.

Chapter 1

TACKLING THE ISSUES

Lighter and sadder

FOR EVERY sort of fly have three; one of a lighter colour, another sadder than the natural fly, and a third of the exact colour with the fly, to suit all waters and weathers, as before.

Robert Venables, *The Experienced Angler*, 1662

✲

Of all the fish that swim the watery mead,
Not one in cunning can the carp exceed.

Daniel Defoe, *Fishing*

Flies – try them under

IN GENERAL, all sorts of flies are very good in their season, for such fish as will rise at the fly, viz. Salmon, Trout, Umber, Grayling, Bleak, Chevin, Roach, Dace, &c. Though some of these fish do love some flies better than other, except the fish named, I know not any sort or kind that will ordinarily and freely rise at the fly, though I know some who angle for Bream and Pike with artificial flies, but I judge the labour lost, and the knowledge a needless curiosity; those fish being taken much easier, especially the Pike, by other ways. All the fore-mentioned sorts of fish will sometimes take the fly much better at the top of the water, and at another time much better a little under the superficies of the water; and in this your own observation must be your constant and daily instructor; for if they will not rise to the top, try them under, it being impossible, in my opinion, to give any certain rule in this particular: also the five sorts of fish first named will take the artificial fly, so will not the other, except an oak-worm or cad-bait be put on the point of the hook, or some other worm suitable, as the fly must be, to the season.

Robert Venables, *The Experienced Angler*, 1662

✵

The fishing rod market worldwide was valued at around $1.1 billion in 2023.

✵

Farlows Fishing Tackle Shop, founded in London in 1838 by Charles Farlow, is the oldest surviving fishing shop in the world.

✵

Horses were once an excellent source of fishing line. Hair taken from the longest horse tails was plaited to make casts – the final few feet of line before the hook. A single hair used for gudgeon fishing and as many as sixteen plaited hairs for barbel fishing.

✵

Cat gut – made from the intestines of cattle, goats and horses – was also used to make casts but, despite its name, it was never made from cat intestines!

✵

Split shot was once made by dropping molten lead from a high tower into cold water.

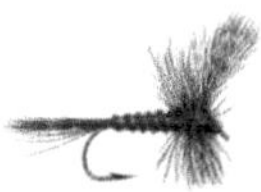

Fish that shoot flies – the jaculator

IN THE Transactions of the Royal Society of London, for 1764, will be found a paper on the Jaculator-fish by Schlosser, the substance of which is extraordinary. When this singular fish (*Chelmon rostratus*) which frequents shores and sides of Indian rivers near the sea in search of food, sees a fly sitting on the plants growing in shallow water, it swims to a distance of five or six feet, and then, with surprising dexterity, it ejects out of its long and tubular mouth a single drop of water, which never fails to strike the fly into the sea, when it becomes its prey.

This aroused Governor Hommel's curiosity, and he had a large tub filled with sea-water, in which he placed some of these fish.

When they were reconciled to their situation, a slender stick with a fly pinned on its end was placed in such a direction on the side of the vessel that the fish could strike it. It was with inexpressible delight that he daily saw these fish exercising their skill in shooting at a fly; and they never missed their mark. Governor Hommel observed that when the Jaculator-fish intends to catch a fly or any other insect which is seen at a distance, it approaches very slowly and cautiously, and comes as much as possible perpendicularly under the object; then the body being put in an oblique position, and the mouth and eyes near the surface of the water, the Jaculator stays a moment quite immovable, having its eyes fixed directly on the insect, and begins to shoot without ever showing its mouth above the surface of the water, out of which the single drop shot at the object seems to rise.

The Jaculator can also shoot flies on the wing and another fish of the same order (*Zeus insidiator*) forms its mouth into a tube and squirts at flies so as to encumber their wings and bring them to the water's surface.

The Angler's Notebook and Naturalist's Record, 1888

✵

The angler envies no man's joys
But his, who gains the greatest sport,
With peace, he dwells far from the noise,
And bustling grandeur of the court.

Anon

Tripod legs

THE CHINESE fisherman, generally seated on a stool with one leg, reminds me of a veteran sportsman noticed by Mr Henderson on the Tweed. On a cold day in the month of April, while fishing for salmon in the Tweed, I once observed a man trouting in a sharp running stream. He lingered there so long that my attention was drawn to him, and seeing that he was without wading boots, I enquired of the boatman how it was possible for a man to remain so long in cold running water. 'Oh, that's old Timbertoes,' was the reply.

'No fear of his feeling the cold. There's nothing like a pair of wooden legs for warmth. But that's not the best of it; look close, and ye'll see he has gotten a third leg which he claps on to his tail and sits down as cozy as if he were in the chimney neuk.' So the mystery was explained; seated on his wooden tripod, the old fellow fished at his ease and drew the trout towards him in true epicurean style.

William Henderson, *Notes and Reminiscences of My Life as an Angler*, 1879

Fish dog

A WATER-SPANIEL, belonging to a gentleman at Lackham, killed all the carp in his master's ponds, and was in consequence condemned to death. Mr Popham, of Littlecot, in the county of Wilts, who had a famous trout-fishery, obtained a reprieve and took charge of the dog, in the belief that so sly and so swift a fish as the trout was not to be caught by a dog. However, in this he was mistaken, for the dog soon convinced him that his largest trout were not a match for him.

William Yarrell, *A History of British Fishes*, 1836

Played by the devil

THE DEVILL I warrant you is perfect in this angling occupation, so he knoweth how to handle a fish hee hath hooked, that he may not

breake from him. Among other trickes that he hath, he will give them time and liberuie, but he will not suffer him to walke further than he list, but he draweth him in again when it best pleaseth him.

Dr Gardiner's Book of Angling, 1606

Spanish poles

Fishing rods, especially longer types including roach poles, were often made from Spanish reed until the early 1960s; the same material is used to make oboe reeds.

✵

A lightweight carbon or boron fly rod cost around £50 to £500 in 2025, but a brand-new split or built cane fly rod from Farlows of Pall Mall would cost at least £1,500.

✵

A Japanese company in the 1980s perfected a reel that would play any hooked fish automatically – the manufacturers were baffled when it didn't take off. They failed to consider that playing a fish using the reel is half the fun of fishing.

Hook making

FRESHWATER HOOK sizes are the wrong way around – the bigger the number, the smaller the hook. For coarse fishing, hooks range from the almost invisible size 26, used for minuscule baits such as bloodworms, to size 2 – used for golf ball dollops of bread or cheese.

Hooks are made from various metal wires, including stainless steel, high-carbon steel, and steel alloyed with vanadium. The wire is cut into desired lengths and straightened. It is then bent and formed into the preferred hook shape, often using a cam or bending tool. The point of the hook is sharpened using files or grinding stones. A barb is sometimes added to the hook, but far less often these days. The hook is heat-treated (tempered) to improve its strength and hardness.

The hook may undergo further finishing processes, such as chemical sharpening or coating with a protective finish.

Wading women

OVER AGAINST Rosse is an Ile named Lewis, sixtie miles in length. In this Ile is but one fresh river, and it is said that if a woman wade through the same, there shall no salmon be seene there for a twelve month after, whereas otherwise that fish is known to abound there in verie great plentie.

Raphael Holinshed, *Chronicles*, 1577

The smell of grayling

IT MAY be owing to the want of a nice olfactory discrimination on my part, but I am unable to connect the odorous emanation of the grayling – said to smell like thyme – with any definite known scent. Others have felt this difficulty. Pennant, for example, denies the existence of any odour.

Still the general opinion is the other way, and it has been suggested that the varying nature of its food may cause the grayling to have at one time a strong odour, which at other seasons, almost, if not entirely disappears. The insects upon which it feeds are some of them highly scented, and would certainly communicate their odour to the fish.

R. S. Manley, *Notes on Fish and Fishing*, 1877

Pike with an eagle's skeleton attached

A CIRCUMSTANCE connected with the size and strength of the pike does not find any place in our fish books. I allude to the contests which frequently occur between large pike and birds of prey.

The sea-eagle and the osprey not unfrequently pounce upon a fish when basking near the surface of the water, and being unable to extricate their crooked talons, a struggle 'to the death' ensues, when they are unable to bear the fish aloft. Mr Lloyd has collected several cases in his *Scandinavian Adventures* (1854), related to him by credible witnesses. He further states that it is not of unusual occurrence to find not only dead pike, but also living fish, with the skeleton of the eagle or the osprey still attached to its back. M. Ekström mentioned finding a pike, not over twenty pounds in weight, with the skeleton of an osprey still attached to it.

The Angler's Notebook and Naturalist's Record, 1888

Sharpe's Scottie

AMONG THE most famous of bamboo fly fishing rods is the Sharpe's Scottie. It features an impregnation process which was used in many rods from a tiny toothpick 7-footer designed for small stream trout to a massive 15ft salmon rod. Impregnation was a process of soaking the cane in a resinous substance that sealed the fibres making them waterproof and stronger.

Tip rings

THE TIP rings on fishing rods (also the butt rings) were traditionally lined with agate – a hard semi-precious stone that prevented the line cutting grooves in its surface.

To be precise, agate is a banded variety of chalcedony, a microcrystalline form of quartz, characterised by its distinctive layered patterns and a range of colours. It's a relatively common gemstone, known for its durability. Agate's colours and patterns are due to the presence of trace elements like iron, manganese, and nickel.

Ceramic and nano plasma rings

MODERN RINGS are lined with ceramic, titanium, silicon carbide, aluminium oxide and even nano plasma. A nano plasma rod ring is made from a material that has been treated with a plasma-coating process. This coating, often PVD (physical vapour deposition) titanium nitride or titanium oxide, is applied to a high-tensile strength, diamond-polished ring, resulting in a near-zero friction surface that allows the fishing line to pass through quickly.

Spliced rods

LONG AFTER brass ferrules (the elements of a rod that enable sections to be fitted tightly together), had replaced spliced rods, the latter were still popular with many older anglers. With a spliced rod the sections that need to be fitted to each other have ends cut on the diagonal. When married up with their counterpart end on the appropriate rod section, the two diagonals fit perfectly together giving the rod a bond at the join that puts the strain across a greater area than is possible with a ferrule. When the diagonals are matched together, they are held together with tape, which is removed at the end of the day so the rod can be dismantled. A small number of salmon anglers were still using cane spliced rods as recently as 2025.

Hinged rings

ON MANY early rods especially greenheart, the rod rings were often just that – rings with no 'legs' to help the line stand away from the rod itself. These early rings were also hinged so they lay flat against the rod when not in use.

The hinge caused the ring to move when the line ran through it, which meant too much friction – far more than in the standout rings that superseded the old rings.

Hardy Bros

STARTING IN the mid-nineteenth century, Hardy Bros produced a wide variety of cane rods. Despite or perhaps because of their reputation for making game fishing rods, they branched out into other spheres: they made split cane avon, carp and barbel rods, split cane fly rods, split cane general, coarse fishing rods, and split cane spinning rods. They also made composite rods, a mixture of greenheart and cane, and whole and built cane composite rods. The Palakona split cane rod, known for its excellence, earned a Gold Medal at the 1883–84 Great Fisheries Exhibition in London.

Hardy Palakona cane rods often came with a concealed metal spike in the butt. That might sound like a weapon but in fact the spike was meant to be removed from the hollow butt, turned round and screwed carefully back into the butt. The idea was that when you paused to change a fly or have a rest from fishing, you weren't tempted to lay the rod on the ground where there was always a danger you might tread on it. With the spike you could push the rod into the ground where it would stand up on its own until you decided to start fishing again. Ingenious, but it never seems to have been taken up by other rod makers.

Set forth your tackle

A MAN that goeth to the River for his pleasure, must understand, when he cometh there, to set forth his Tackles. The first thing he must do, is to observe the Sun, the Wind, the Moon, the Starres, and the Wanes of the Air; to set forth his Tackles according to the times and seasons; to goe for his pleasure, and some profit.

As for example, the Sun proves cloudy; then must he set forth either his ground Bait or Tackles, and of the brightest of his Flies. If the Sun prove bright, then must he put on some of the darkest of his flies. Thus must you goe to work with your Flies, light for darkness, and dark for lightness, with the wind in the South, then that blows the Flie in the Trout's mouth. Though I set down the wind being in the South, if the weather be warm, I am indifferent where the wind standeth, either with ground Bait or Menow, so that I can cast my Bait into the River. The very same observations is for night, as for day: For if the Moon prove cleer, or if the Stars glitter in the skie, there is as ill Angling that night, as if it were at high noon in the midst of Summer, when the Sun shineth at the brightest, wherein there is no hopes of pleasure.

Thomas Barker, *The Art of Angling*, 1651

Three haired links

THE FIRST thing you must gaine, must be a neat taper Rod, light before, with a tender hazell top, which is very gentle. If you desire to attain my way of Angling, (for I have Angled these forty years) with a single haire of five lengths, one tied to another for the bottom of my Line, and a Line of three haired links for the uppermost part; and so you may catch the greatest Trout that swims, with Sea-room.

He that Angles with a Line made of three haired links at the bottom, and more at the top, may kill Fish: but he that Angles with one hair shall kill five Trouts to the other's one; for the Trout is very quick sighted; therefore the best way for night or day, is to keep out of the sight. You must Angle alwayes with the point of your Rod downe the stream; for a Fish hath not the quickness of sight so perfect up the stream, as opposite against him, observing seasonable times; as for example, we begin to Angle in March. If it prove cloudie, you may Angle with the ground Baits all day long: but if it prove bright and cleere, you must take the morning and evening, or else you are not like to do any good; so the times must be observed, and truely understood; for when an Angler commeth to the River for his pleasure that doth not understand to set forth his Tackles fit for the time, it is as good keep them in the bag, as set them forth.

I am determined to Angle with the ground Baits and set my Tackles to my Rod, and go to my pleasure: I begin at the uppermost part of the streame, carrying my Line with an upright hand, feeling the Plummet running on the ground some ten inches from the hook, plumming my Line according to the swiftnesse of the stream you Angle in; for one plummet will not serve for all streams; for the true Angling is that the plummet runneth on the ground.

For the Bait. The red knotted worme is very good where Brandlings are not to be had, but Brandlings are better: now that you may bring these Brandlings fit to Angle with, that they may live long on the hook, which causeth the best sport. When you have gathered your worms out of the dung-hill, you must gaine the greenest Moss you can find, then wash the earth very clean out of it, then provide an earthen pot, so put your Moss into the pot, then put the worms to the Moss into the pot; within two days you shall find your worms so poor, that if you bait some of them on your hook, you shall see that with throwing of them two or three times into the water, they will dye and grow white: now the skill is, when these worms be grown poor, you must feed them up to make them fat and lusty, that they may live long on the hook; that is the chiefest point.

To make them lusty and fat, you must take the yolke of an Egge, some eight or ten spoonfull of the top of new milk, beaten well together in a Porringer, warm it a little, untill you see it curdle; then take it off the fire, and set it to coole; when it is cold, take a spoonfull and drop it upon your Moss into the pot, every drop about the bignesse of a green Pea, shifting your Moss twice in the week in the Summer, and once in the winter: thus doing, you shall feed your wormes fat, and make them lusty, that they will live a long time on the hook; so you may keep them all the year long. This is my true experience for the ground Baits, for the running Line for the Trout.

Robert Venables, *The Experienced Angler*, 1662

Use shoemaker's wax to your silk or thread, with which you make or mend either rod or fly; it holds firmer, and sticks better than any other.

Robert Venables, *The Experienced Angler*, 1662

Burnt nets

BE IT remembered, that on the Wednesday next before the Feast of Easter, that is to say, on the Feast of St Alphage [19 April, in the 3rd year of the reign of King Edward the Third] there came Estmar Coker and John Wychard, citizens of London, together with Ralph Bourghard, Serjeant of the Chamber of Guildhall, and brought before the Mayor and Aldermen, at the Guildhall, John Jacob of Erhitthe [Erith], Edmund Dode of Reynham, Thomas Wychard of Erhitthe, William Niece of Stokflete, Robert Scof of Erhitthe, John Noreys of Erhitthe, Alan le Spenser of Reynham, and Alexander of Dagenham, fisherman; for that they had been found fishing in the water of Thames with twelve nets which are known as tromekeresnet and are a kind of kidel: the meshes of which nets, which are called mascles, ought to be one inch and a half in size, whereas they were hardly half an inch; and with which nets the said fishermen caught every fish, and every little fish even, that entered such nets. By reason whereof, the small fish, which are called fry, were unable to escape or get out of the said nets; to the great damage of all the people of the city, and also of others unto the same city resorting. And the said John Jacob and others, being questioned as to this, did not deny it, nor could they deny that they had done as before stated, to the loss, &c. It was therefore ordered by the Mayor and Aldermen that the said nets should be burnt at the Cross in Chepe; and the said fishermen committed to prison, until they should have made fine, &c. And they were accordingly delivered to the Sheriff in form aforesaid and taken to Newgate.

Afterwards, on the Saturday next after the Invention of the Holy Cross [3 May], they were brought to the Guildhall before the Mayor and Aldermen, from the prison aforesaid; and by assent of such Mayor and Aldermen, by special favour and for charity's sake, seeing that they were but poor men, the fines were remitted to them for the present; on the understanding that they should behave themselves well for the future, and no longer presume to fish with such nets.

Henry Riley (tr.), *Memorials of London and London Life in the 13th, 14th and 15th Centuries*, 1868

Line making

To make the Line
Good hayre then get, so that it be not blacke;
Neither of Mare nor Gelding let it be;
Nor of the tyreling jade that beares the packe:
But of some lusty Horse or Courser free,
Whose bushie tayle upon the ground doth tracke
Like blazing Comete that sometimes we see:
From out the mid'st thereof the longest take,
At leysure best your Linkes and Lines to make.

John Dennys, *The Secrets of Angling*, 1613

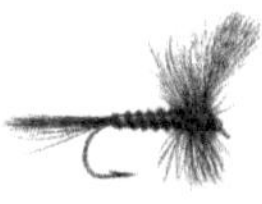

Boat sail coats

THE MUCH-LOVED wax angling coat – gradually now being superseded by Gore-Tex and other hi-tech materials – started life in a most curious way. It evolved from boat sails. These were treated with oil to waterproof them and it must have seemed a natural progression to make waterproof coats out of the same oiled sailcloth. Sails were treated with fish oil and later linseed oil to waterproof them and the idea was simply adapted for clothing, with the earliest wax coats actually being made from remnants of old sails.

Match the hatch

MANY ACCOMPLISHED anglers, and authors as well, are under the impression that on every river, certain peculiar flies will be more alluring to trout all the season through, than any others that can be offered them. This mistaken notion is most prevalent with southern sportsmen, where the rivers are ill-adapted to fly fishing, and where that mode of fishing is but seldom followed and little understood. As a case in point – in *Fly fishing* by Ephemera, not one of the flies in his list, with but one solitary exception, the dark dun, has the slightest resemblance to any aquatic insect that God ever created; nor in the clear oft-fished waters of the North, would they have ever an ephemeral chance of filling a basket at any season of the year. My own opinion, derived from long experience and a close attention to the matter, most decidedly compels me to arrive at the conclusion, that unless the artificial flies resemble as closely their natural prototypes frequenting the waters at the season fished in as the art of the dresser can make them, the angler may as well remain at home, and whip for imaginary whales in his wash-hand basin.

A. S. Moffat, *The Secrets of Angling*, 1885

Angling magazines no longer with us

The Angler's News, *Angling* magazine, *Coarse Fishing Monthly*, *Sea Angling Monthly*, *Stillwater Trout Angler*, *Angler's Mail*, *Coarse Angling*, *Improve Your Sea Fishing*, and many others too numerous to mention.

Still going strong: *Angling Times*, published without a break since the early 1950s; *Trout & Salmon* founded in 1955.

Bite while washing

WHEN SHEPHERDS or countrymen wash their sheep, though while they are washing, I mean the first time only, the fish will bite exceedingly well; I suppose the filth that falls from the sheep draws them, as like baiting a place together, and then they so glut themselves, that till the whole washing time be over, and they have digested their fulness; they will not take any artificial baits.

Robert Venables, *The Experienced Angler*, 1662

Give the eel time

THERE ARE two ways of fishing for Eels, proper and peculiar to that fish alone; the first is termed by some, angling for Eels, which is thus: take a short strong rod, and exceeding strong line, with a little compassed, but strong hook, which you must bait with a large well-scoured red worm, then place the end of the hook very easily in a cleft of a stick, that it may very easily slip out; with this stick and hook thus baited, search for holes under stones, timbers, roots, or about floodgates; if there be a good Eel, give her time, and she will take it; but be sure she has gorged it, and then you may conclude, if your tackling hold, she is your own.

Robert Venables, *The Experienced Angler*, 1662

Pike and goose

THE PRINCIPALL sport to take a Pike, is to take a Goose or Gander, or Duck: take one of the Pike Lines I have shewed you before: tye the Line under the left wing, and over the right wing, about the body, as a man weareth his Belt: turne the Goose off into a Pond, where *Pikes* are, there is no doubt of sport, with great pleasure, betwixt the Goose and the *Pike*: It is the greatest sport and pleasure that a noble Gentleman in *Shropshire* doth give his friends entertainment with.

Thomas Barker, *The Art of Angling*, 1651

All kinds of rods

IN RESPECT to fly-rods, I believe the London tackle-makers can furnish as good as any that are made for sale; though I know some Gentlemen are partial to those manufactured in the North and West parts of England. I have purchased rods at Exeter for fishing in the river Ex, the Tamar, and other Trout streams in Devonshire, in compliance with the request of some friends who reside in those parts; but I never experienced any advantage in using them over what I carried with me from the metropolis.

Fly-rods are made of bamboo, cane, hickory, hazel, &c. from fifteen to eighteen feet long; the common hazel rod may be used by the young Angler, during his noviciate, to practise throwing a fly on land, in a field, or any other convenient place, which practice I should recommend before he casts his bait on the water. While so practising, it is better to break away the point and barb of the hook, to prevent its laying hold of grass, weeds, or anything that may be in the way, which would either break the line, or prevent the fly being thrown with any precision.

… and lines

are manufactured of hair, &c., wove, spun, twisted, mixed, and platted, of various lengths and strengths, purposely for fly fishing; some exceedingly fine and long, tapering gradually to the end; and some, after ten yards, again taper, and to almost any length; a line should not be less than thirty yards. A yard or two of fine gut, to which the hooks are fastened, is added to the line, and called the bottom. To the end of this bottom is fastened the fly; and sometimes, at certain distances, (above) two more; in which case the fly at the bottom is termed the stretcher, the others droppers. The learner should by no means attempt to fish with more than one fly on at a time. When fly fishing, use as light a winch as you can, but always prefer the multiplying one.

Thomas Salter, *Art of Angling*, 1833

Types of hook

- Spade end
- Eyed
- Dublin bend
- Treble
- Stiff rigger
- Chod
- Aberdeen

Float fishing methods:

- Lift fishing
- Stret-pegging
- Waggler fishing
- Stick float
- Trotting

Inventing monofilament

NYLON MONOFILAMENT is the most commonly used fishing line in the UK. Invented by an American company – Dupont – in the 1930s, nylon monofilament can be immensely strong yet remain thin and translucent. When it was first introduced many anglers felt it gave them an unfair advantage and as a result silk lines for some kinds of fishing are still used today.

Monofilament also has its downsides: it enabled commercial fishermen to make cheap nets which could be stretched for miles across sections of ocean. All well and good so long as the nets weren't lost. Gill nets, as these are called, if lost continue to fish for years on the bottom of the sea; as fish get caught by their gills the nets become heavier until they are weighed down to the ocean floor. Then as the caught fish rot, the nets float up and begin again to kill fish.

… he [the tench] inclines very much to any paste with which tar has been mixt.

Izaak Walton, *The Compleat Angler*, 1653

Wife or fishing?

A CERTAIN Vicar of Thames Ditton … went gudgeon fishing on his wedding morning to while away the time and 'whiled' away too much of it! On arriving – late – at the church, the lady, a daughter of the then Bishop of London, in a fit of indignation, turned him down, refusing to marry a man 'preferring his basket to his bride'!

Faddist, *Memorable Coarse Fish*, 1953

Electric disturbance

WHEN THE electrical equilibrium of the atmosphere is at all disturbed, it is in general absurd to try fly fishing.

John Kirkbride, 1840, Quoted in
Trout Heresy by P. B. M. Allan, 1936

Casting with a centrepin

THERE IS a streak in the average British sportsman which gives him a craving for doing things tip-top and up to date.

In angling, the art of float casting from the reel has reached a very high standard of skill and is undoubtedly the most effective and graceful of all the methods of getting the float a big distance from the bank or boat, and this with a minimum of effort and preparation. It entirely eliminates all forms of the pulling of loops from the rings of rod, or that of coiling the line on the ground previous to making a cast.

Seventy or eighty years ago some form of casting from the reel was practised by two Nottingham celebrities: William Bailey who was considered the cleverest angler of his day and who won many prizes against all comers; the other angler was the redoubtable Bendigo, the champion prize-fighter of England. These two sportsmen did, to a certain extent, use this cast in a modified and limited sense, but as rods at that time were heavy and clumsy and the reels of very primitive make, the cast was limited to 50 or 60ft.

Another fatal disadvantage was that the angler, in making the cast, left the float and cast swinging loose from the top of the rod and it was manipulated in the same style as when pike fishing with live bait; therefore, the cast was out of the question where trees, bushes, or tall reeds and sedges were either to the right or left of the angler.

Fishing in the following style, the angler who has the art thoroughly mastered will have no difficulty in propelling the float to a distance of 100ft and this with an easy grace and very little effort. It matters not if there are trees or other natural obstructions to the right or left, so long as there is open water in front and the length of the rod clear on either side.

This cast is made with equal facility when sitting on the bank or when seated on the creel or stool. It is an easy swing with an entire absence of snatch or jerk, and the cast is so smooth that even a grain of well-creneled wheat will remain on a No. 12 hook when making a 100ft cast and fishing 12ft deep.

The rod is firmly held in the right hand by the first three fingers and thumb, leaving the little finger free to act as a very delicate brake or check on the top rim of the reel. The tackle is also shown held by the fingers of the left hand; the thumb being looped over the line from reel. The rod is now brought forward and nearly horizontal and parallel with the left shoulder, the little finger of the right hand holds the reel in check; the rod is now brought forward with a firm but easy sweep, and at the same time the line is pulled off the reel backwards to the full extent of the left arm.

The momentum contributed by the swing of the rod propels the float forward quicker than the eye can follow, the little finger of the right hand has released the drum of the reel and at the psychological moment the line running over the thumb of the left hand is brought forward, down goes the little finger on the reel as the cast is completed and the float alights on the water 100ft away.

Of course, the timing of this cast must be as accurate as that of a six-cylinder engine in a motorcar, but once mastered it is simplicity itself. The best methods for the learner to adopt being to follow the above suggestions and get just a few yards away to begin with, then to add an extra yard or two every time until the full distance is attained.

H. T. Sheringham, *An Open Creel*, 1910

Leaving the roach

WASN'T IT in H. W.'s book on roach fishing, where somewhere on the Lea he was catching roach like steam – pounders every one – when towards dark, though the fish bit as well as ever, someone persuaded him to leave off, which, as he said, he did like a fool, and had never been happy since.

It would be a pretty tall friend, by the way, who would get me to leave off if the fish were taking.

Izaak Walton sayeth, 'I envy not him that eats better meat than I do, nor him that is richer, or wears better clothes than I do. I envy but him, and him only, that catches more fish than I do.'

Francis Francis, *Reminiscences*, 1887

Chapter 2

TAKING THE BAIT

Blowing of brains

THE BAITS for Chub are greaves, gentles, paste, red worms, bullock's brains, and pith from the backbone.

You may, occasionally, take heavy Chub with a lobworm, either laid as a peg-line, at night time, or with a leger in the day. Chub are also sometimes taken with a Roach or Gudgeon, when trolling for Jack.

Trolling or angling with a live minnow or a small frog is also often successfully practised, particularly in the latter end of Spring, by which method many large Chub are taken. (Troll the same as for Trout.) During April and May, red worms are a good bait; two should be put on the hook, the same as for Barbel; for the Chub loves a large bait. In the Summer months, gentles and greaves, but during Summer and Autumn, greaves are the best bait; during Winter and in March, bullock's brains and pith is a killing bait.

To bait with bullock's brains and pith, observe the following rules:– take some pith of the backbone of an ox, and cut it into small pieces, nearly the size of a cherry, to bait the hook. The bullock's brains are to be chewed, and spit out of your mouth into the water, as ground-bait to entice the Chub. Plumb the depth, and fish close to the bottom; you may catch some at mid-water or a little lower, but more at bottom; this method is practised during the Winter, when Chub retire to deep still holes, where you must angle for them, and fear not taking very heavy Fish, for, at this season, Chub are immoderately fond of the above bait.

Note, chewing and spitting out the brains into the water for ground-bait, is called blowing of brains; but as many Anglers feel great objection or antipathy to the chewing of raw brains, they should prepare them as follows: take as many bullock's, cow's, calf's, or sheep's brains as will nearly fill a quart pan, cut them into small pieces with a pair of scissors and if you then pound them in a mortar, afterwards, it will be better; now mix the brains carefully with bran and some house sand, and cast them into the water, in small quantities, and repeat it occasionally while you are angling.

Edward Jesse, *An Angler's Rambles*, 1836

The warm-blooded fish

ATLANTIC BLUEFIN tuna – the species beloved by the Japanese and used in the best sushi and sashimi – grow to around 6ft in length and weigh as much as 1,500lb. The record rod-caught fish as of 2025 weighed 1,496lb (679kg), and was caught by Ken Fraser off Nova Scotia, Canada, in October 1979. Bluefin are continuously on the move and are voracious feeders eating almost anything that moves and even filter feeding when food is scarce. All species of tuna are also remarkable in that they are warm blooded.

Bluefin tuna need more than ten times the amount of food per pound of their weight compared to salmon.

Parchment

TAKE SO much parchment as will be about four inches broad, and five long, make the longer end round, then take so many pieces more as will make five or six partitions, sew them all together, leaving the side of the longest square open, to put your lines, spare links, hooks ready fastened, and flies ready made, into the several partitions; this will contain much, and will also lie flat and close in your pocket.

Robert Venables, *The Experienced Angler*, 1662

In Flanders, the inside of a red cherry contains the most killing bait for chub.

T. F. Salter, *The Angler's Guide*, 1815

Winter gentles

GENTLES, OR maggots, may be bred from any animal substance, either fish, flesh, or fowl, (those from fish are least worthy) by exposing it to flies to blow on during the Spring and Summer. (I have found flies in Winter, among ivy, in walls that are fronting the South; and, on a warm day, have procured them; by which means, I have had flesh blown by flies, and bred gentles in every month during Winter.) After they are of a full size, put them in a vessel, with some house-sand; some use bran, but, from its heating quality, the gentles sooner turn, as Anglers term it, that is, become a chrysalis, in which state they are of little or no use.

In London, it is not worth the trouble of breeding gentles, for as many as will serve a day's fishing may be purchased at any of the tackle-shops for a few pence.

The least troublesome method I am acquainted with, to keep gentles during the Winter, is to get some full-grown ones, as late in the season as possible, and put them with fresh mould, and half-dried cow-dung, into a vessel two or three feet in depth, which vessel must be kept in a cool cellar or out-house, occasionally sprinkling a little water over them; by adopting this plan, I am seldom without gentles in February, March, and April, in which months they are a valuable bait. When you use any at this season of the year, (during the Spring) take only as many as you are likely to want, and keep them cool and close, or they will soon turn to a chrysalis, if exposed to the air; therefore, close immediately up the place you take them from: for want of attending to this caution, many lose their preserved stock in a few days.

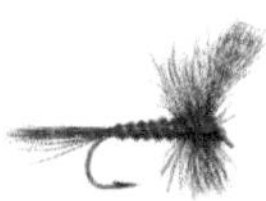

In the Summer season, when on a fishing excursion from home, I take a quantity of gentles, rather green, with me, and daily give them a small piece of fresh flesh or liver, or a small fish; the small gentles then increase in size, and keep up my stock of a proper size.

When you go out for a day's angling with gentles, put them in sand or earth, rather damp; for, if put in a box with bran, they may turn brown. – Note. Carp, Tench, Barbel, and Chub, prefer gentles that are somewhat green; they are then of a higher flavour and scent, which is very enticing to most Fish.

Anglers who live in the country may, if they choose, breed and preserve gentles all the year in the following manner: get the whole, or part of a bullock's liver, in October, or the heads of sheep, with part of the wool on; cut gashes in them, and let them be well blown by the flies. When the fly-blows are become full-grown gentles, put them, and the remains of the liver, or heads, into a tight cask or tub, having first put into the tub or cask about a peck of fresh mould from the fields; to which add half the quantity of half-dried cow-dung, and then put the same quantity of mould and dung over them; keep them in a cool place, and when the mould, &c., at the top, becomes dry, sprinkle a little water over it. Using liver or heads, I think less disagreeable than having a dead animal blown on by flies; but those who prefer a rabbit or hare, or cat or dog, have only to follow the directions given above, and they will have gentles at all times. Those who may object to keep the gentles in the house may preserve them in the garden, by putting the liver, or other substance, with the gentles, mould, or dung, in a hole about three feet deep; but note, this hole must be plastered round and at bottom with strong clay, or the gentles will penetrate into the earth, to a great distance. I find those bred from rabbits, hares, or heads, less likely to burrow in the earth, because the skin and wool keeps longer moist, and also affords them food. When you open the store do it carefully, for when the cool Spring air reaches the gentles, they quickly become a chrysalis. Horse-dung is too hot for gentles, but cow-dung nourishes them, as will hogs'-dung also, but in a less degree.

The best way to keep gentles, in the Summer, is to put them in a salmon kit, (which may be bought of the people who sell pickled salmon,) with some house-sand, and sprinkle daily a handful of dampish sand over them, or a very little water, and they will keep from changing to a chrysalis much longer than if kept in a box or bag; for the kit being very broad at the bottom, enables the gentles to move about and keep themselves cool: but when they are laid on each other, in heaps, in a box or bag, they soon become heated, and consequently soon change to the chrysalis state. As gentles are so valuable a bait, the Angler should not object taking a little trouble to keep them. I have tried many ways, and the above directions are the result of my experience.

Thomas Salter, *The Art of Angling*, 1833

Tar and tench?

THEY [tench] prefer worms to any other bait, though sometimes a bunch of gentles will be found to tempt them; a red worm, however, is their favourite bait, and, with a No. 7 hook and a couple of red worms neatly strung on, the angler should take tench if they are inclined to feed at all.

I remember formerly to have read that it was a good plan to dip the red worm in tar, but I cannot believe it, as tar is usually death to fish of all kinds, and utterly abhorrent to them; but the old writers were fond of strange theories, many of which I have proved to be utterly false.

Francis Francis, *A Book on Angling*, 1867

*

The nineteenth-century angling writer H. Cholmondeley-Pennell records a trout eating a swallow.

Rat-eating trout

'THE LARGER fish in our chalk stream,' writes a Hampshire fisherman in 1916, 'are very broad-minded in the matter of food. Bread, gentles, dead eels, eel skins, and their heads, the young of the water fowl, a frog, and the smaller water rats have all appeared in the menu.

'That trout prey upon the newly hatched moorhens and dabchicks there is no doubt,' continues the same observer. 'I have seen two instances of it. In the first case I believe the victim was a baby moorhen, but the second was without any question a tiny dabchick. The

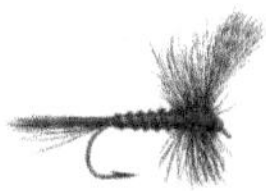

trout was quite close to me, and I could clearly see the peculiar foot of the dabchick sticking out at the side of the fish's mouth; and the foot and leg appeared to move as if the victim had only just been taken.' Mr Nicoll then records three cases of rat-eating trout which he personally has seen in Hampshire. He also describes a frog-eating trout – he watched him for some time trying without success to make a meal of a dead and bloated frog, which the trout could not pull to pieces.

P. B. M. Allan, *Trout Heresy*, 1936

Bogus trout

THROUGHOUT THE centuries, fishermen have regarded the trout as a sagacious animal possessed of great cunning. It is a comfortable doctrine ... but entirely bogus.

P. B. M. Allan, *Trout Heresy*, 1936

Eating anything

THE TROUT so they say, 'exhibits a remarkable degree of nicety and fastidiousness about his food'. Alas, the autopsy of a trout is sufficient to disprove this. According to Francis Day's 1887 study, *British and Irish Salmonidae*, the trout eats 'minnows, loach, sticklebacks, water rats, young birds, frogs, snails, slugs, worms, leeches, maggots, flies, beetles, moths, water spiders, and even a lizard'.

It will also eat its own species, as well as water insects and everything that lives and moves.

Strike too soon

STRIKE SMARTLY but not too heavily, when you feel a touch, and not before – indeed feeling should supersede seeing in this matter, and the less you see the better. I once saw a seven-pound Thames trout come at my bait at Sunbury; I saw his great white mouth open, and the bait disappear, and I struck. I felt nothing at all, the bait uninjured came one way, and the trout of course went another. If I had not seen that fish, I most likely would have waited till I felt him, when I should have hooked him. But to this day I never can make out how it was I did not hook, or even touch him, when I saw a bait with ten or eleven hooks on it disappear apparently into his cavernous mouth.

Francis Francis, *A Book on Angling*, 1867

Mostly gone

ONLY 10 per cent of historic stocks of large sea fish – marlin, swordfish, tuna and sharks remain.

Poetic fly-tying

To frame the little animal, provide,
All the gay hues that wait on female pride.
Let nature guide thee; sometimes, golden wire
The shining bellies of the fly require;
The peacock plumes thy tackle must not fail,
Nor the drear purchase of the sable's tail.
Each gaudy bird some slender tribute brings,
And lends the growing insect proper wings:
Silks, of all colours, must their aid impart,
And every fur promote the fisher's art.
So the gay lady, with expensive care,
Borrows the pride of land, of sea, and air;
Furs, pearls, and plumes the glittering thing displays,
Dazzles our eyes, and easy hearts betrays.

John Gay, *Rural Sports*, 1713

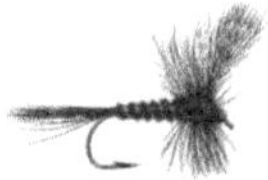

Eels from dead bodies (according to Virgil)

PLINY'S THEORY was, that when eels had lived their day they instinctively rubbed themselves to pieces against the rocks, and that out of the living detritus issued a new brood: a mode of generation which in some lower animal organizations actually takes place. Many as implicitly believed this ingenious hypothesis, as children duly instructed believe that an effete moon is cut up into stars, and that the monthly succession of old ones has gradually been filling the sky with these lesser luminaries ever since the world began to the present hour.

Some, dissatisfied with such explanations, observing how easily Virgil contrived to fill his bee-hives from the carcase of a heifer, and not seeing why if bees were so generated fish might not be also, affirmed that eels came from the dead bodies of animals after long immersion in water.

Others again modified this notion, and supposed that only the hairs of a horse's tail, soaked a sufficient time, would at last adapt themselves to a new element and become eels. Finally, some ancient naturalists, finding the terrestrial origin of eels obscure, had recourse to the skies, and attributed this multitudinous race to Jupiter and a white-armed goddess named Anguilla; accordingly, Archestratus, in his description of an Attic feast, introduces Anguilla, boasting of her Jove-sprung offspring.

In much later times, Van Helmont attributed the birth of eels to the dews of May mornings.

The Angler's Notebook and Naturalist's Record, 1888

Local names

PEEL, FINNOCK, herling, whitling, sewin, and white trout are all regional names for sea trout.

Slobs

TROUT THAT start heading for the sea and then change their minds are known as slob trout.

Gulping air

ON A summer evening carp and tench break the surface of the water with their leathery mouths and gulp down air. I have never known barbel to do this.

Francis Ward, *Marvels of Fish Life*, 1911

Experiments with trout

EXPERIMENT I. He lowered a weighted artificial fly in various places a number of times. No trout were attracted.

Experiment II. He soaked the fly in beef blood and lowered it again. In less than half a minute several trout came towards the fly and one of 1lb took it and was hooked and landed. The experiment was repeated in several places, always with a similar result, except, I suppose, concerning the weight of the captured fish.

Experiment III. He lowered a line to which three lures were attached, three feet apart. These lures were: (1) a small piece of raw beef an inch square; (2) a piece of pork the same size; (3) a fly without hook soaked in beef blood. Result: four trout immediately went for the beef and one got it, another trout made for the fly after the beef was taken; no trout took the pork, though two nosed it. The experiment was repeated several times with the same results, except that once a 5lb trout took the pork.

Experiment IV. Five lures on the line, viz.: (1) a piece of beef; (2) a fly soaked in beef blood; (3) a piece of liver; (4) an angle worm; (5) the entrails of a small trout. No trout were in sight when the line was lowered. Result: the beef was taken before it reached the bottom; the fly before it reached the bottom but after the beef; the liver as it reached the bottom; the worm thirty seconds after it had been wriggling on the bottom; the entrails not until the other lures had been taken.

The experiment was repeated several times, and there was practically no variation in the results.

P. B. M. Allan, *Trout Heresy*, 1936

Horn bait

WHILE I have not, like Mr Haskins, 'caught many trout with artificial baits made of horn,' I can vouch that in England horn minnows still exist and that horn spoons are even now used for pike.

William Radcliffe, *Fishing from the Earliest Times*, 1921

✵

The Japanese puffer fish draws complex geometric patterns in the sand to attract a mate.

Surviving drought

THE AUSTRALIAN lungfish can survive for years buried in a ball of its own mucous when its home river or lake has completely dried up. When the rains come, the fish come back to life.

Fierce

MALE STICKLEBACKS build a nest to attract females. The males then fiercely guard the nests until the eggs hatch.

No herrings

DESPITE BEING one of the world most populous fish, herrings are almost never caught by anglers.

✵

Fish were the first animals to evolve bony skeletons more than 450 million years ago.

✵

Eels only spawn in the Sargasso Sea near Bermuda, which means British eels must travel up to 6,000 miles to reproduce. It can take three years for newly hatched eels to swim this distance back to the UK.

Giant catfish

THE WELS catfish is an introduced species to the UK. It has roughly 27,000 taste buds compared to 7,000 in humans. The biggest catfish ever caught on rod and line in the UK, as of 2025, weighed a staggering 150lb. Wels can reach seventy years of age.

✵

Only one UK freshwater fish can swim backwards – the common eel.

How eels survive being swallowed

JAPANESE EELS have been recorded breaking out of a predator's stomach, by moving tail-first up the fish's digestive tract, then squeezing their way out through its gills. A team in Japan recorded thirty-two eels being captured and swallowed by a dark sleeper fish. X-ray imagery showed the eels escaping through the sleeper fish's gills. The eels could be seen swimming around in the fish's stomach, seemingly looking for an escape route. Nine found one, and successfully escaped.

✵

Rod and line fishing accounts for less than 1 per cent of the total annual spearfish catch worldwide.

✵

The highest price ever paid for a tuna was $3.1 million (333.6 million yen) for a 278kg bluefin tuna in 2019 at the first pre-dawn New Year's auction in Tokyo's new fish market.

A shark's liver makes up 30 per cent of its body mass – the liver is filled with a light oil, which aids buoyancy as sharks don't have a swim bladder.

Famous angling writers, singers and artists

- Ernest Hemingway
- George Orwell
- Feargal Sharkey
- Rita Ora
- Ted Hughes
- Arthur Ransome
- Eric Clapton
- Roger Daltrey
- Brandi Carlile
- Avril Lavigne

Ridiculous receipts

PASTE IS a killing and general bait for almost every kind of Fish that breed in rivers or any fresh waters, but it requires some little time and labour to make it, which must be done with clean hands; also care and skill in using it. Many strange and ridiculous receipts are to be met with for making paste, which tend much to confound and puzzle the inexperienced Angler; such as part of the leg of a kitten, with bees' wax, suet, &c., beat up in a mortar; or cherries and cheese, sheep's blood and saffron; or cheese, flour, dead men's fat, aniseed water, and roasted bacon: many others, equally useless and absurd, I could mention; but I shall better serve the novice in angling, by assuring him, that nothing more is wanted in making paste to kill every kind of Fish, which will take paste, than flour-bread, water, and honey, (with a little vermilion or red ochre to colour the paste, which may sometimes be useful) and teaching him how to make and use the same.

Thomas Salter, *The Art of Angling*, 1833

Greaves

GREAVES ARE the protein-containing residues that remain after animal fat, including bones, is rendered. This process involves melting the fat for human consumption, and the greaves are the solid, fibrous matter left behind. They are also known as cracklings. Formerly they were an excellent bait for chub.

The shoemaker tench

A GOOD way of serving tench is, cooked in a rich gravy sauce, containing raisins, Corinth currants, and pine-cone kernels … bringing it quite hot to table, and there squeezing over it the juice of a lemon: or else take just sufficient water to cover the fish, add a quarter of a pint of vinegar, a bunch of thyme, an onion, some lemon-peel, a little scraped horse-radish, and a seasoning of salt; put in the tench before the water boils, to prevent the skin cracking: for sauce, dissolve two anchovies in water over the fire, with half a pint of stewed oysters, a quarter of a pint of shrimps, and a sufficient quantity of melted butter; garnish the dish with slices of lemon and pickled mushrooms.

The skin (which from its thickness has procured this fish in Holland the name of shoemaker) is a first-rate delicacy, and quite equal to turtle.

Charles Badham, *Fish Tattle*, 1854

Dancing Float

In flow'ry meads, oh let me live!
Where crystal streams sweet solace give;

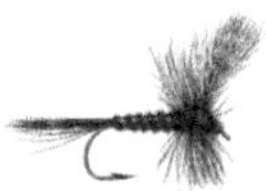

To whose harmonious bubbling sound,
My dancing float and heart rebound.

John Dennys, *The Secrets of Angling*, 1613

Gut feeling

THE CATERPILLAR of the silkworm, at a certain stage of its existence, spins around it a fine silken cocoon (the silk of commerce), in which it passes the aurelia or chrysalis state, preparatory to its issuing again into the world transformed into a winged moth.

Now just previous to the commencement of this cocoon, which may be known by the caterpillar ceasing to eat, and while the body of the grub is replete with the silky secretion, they are killed by a momentary immersion in boiling water; and on laying hold of each extremity and pulling the body of the grub moderately, it will generally separate near the centre, and disclose to view a greenish white coloured gut, which is not an intestine, but the organ which secretes the silky matter for the purpose of forming the cocoon.

This gut-like organ is taken by the extremities, and gradually extended until the requisite length and tenuity are obtained, when the ends are wound round wire pins fixed along each side of a board of the proper width; then exposed to dry and consolidate in the air and sunshine.

Of course, the greater the extension, the longer and finer the lengths of the gut will be; while the kind known as salmon-gut is comparatively thick and short, from being less extended than that used for trouting purposes.

Gut of both kinds ought to be as round and smooth as wire; and for trout-lines it cannot almost be too fine, provided it is round and even. Gut of this description is incredibly strong compared to its dimensions. I never use gut for fly fishing thicker than a fine horse-hair, and yet it is so sound and strong that I will undertake to kill any fish under three pounds with it by proper management.

I may observe that nine-tenths of the gut offered for sale in the shops is flat, uneven, and of very inferior quality; and I would not accept of a waggon-load of it as a gift.

Edward Jesse, *An Angler's Rambles*, 1836

Fennel baits

THE OLD writers were fond of strange theories, many of which I have proved to be utterly false. I once spoilt a capital day's trouting by keeping my worms in fennel by the advice of some old writer – perhaps he had our friend Greville in his mind, and not the herb of that name – which did not agree with the fish at all; for they no sooner took it in their mouths than they spat it out again in apparent disgust, and I lost scores of good bites, till I had at last to hunt for others in a pelting rain, when I did better – bad as the substitute was.

Francis Francis, *A Book on Angling*, 1867

Viviparous

SHARKS GIVE birth to live young – i.e. they are viviparous – so too do many popular aquarium fish include platies, mollies and guppies.

Deadly meal

PUFFER FISH contain the deadly toxin tetrodotoxin. Despite this the Japanese eat them – there are highly trained chefs who know exactly which parts of the puffer fish are safe to eat. But every year mistakes are made and people die.

So what is the appeal? Well, eaten in just the right quantity fugu – to use the Japanese word – make the diner feel slightly lightheaded and numb, a feeling not dissimilar to the effects of alcohol.

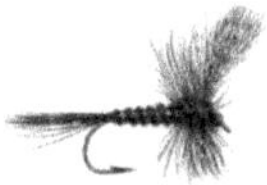

Shark tooth

A FOSSILISED shark tooth 7in long is the biggest ever found – it probably came from a megalodon, which probably measured more than 50ft long.

✵

The great white shark has 300 teeth in seven rows.

✵

Pharyngeal teeth are located in the pharyngeal arch (throat) of certain fish species, most especially cyprinids which includes in the UK, tench, bream, carp and chub.

Sparing the tench

The pike, fell tyrant of the liquid plain,
Howsoe'er by raging famine pined,
The tench he spares – a medicinal kind;
For when, by wounds distrest and sore disease,
He courts the salutary fish for ease,
Close to his scales the kind physician glides,
And sweats a healing balsam from his sides.

Moses Brown, *Piscatory Eclogues*, 1729

Feeding roach

AN INSTANCE of the effect of food supply on roach. A pond swarmed with small roach (there are many such little waters); never a sizeable fish to be caught there. Ninety-nine of these roach were captured and transferred to another pool of a different type, containing no fish whatsoever, a bare three hundred yards away. This latter pool was shallow and muddy; the cattle drank from it and on hot days stood in it. It formed the home of millions of blood-worms; good feeding for roach. Four years later the owner fished therein and quickly captured six roach aggregating exactly 5lb.

Game and Gun, 1950

One thousand tonnes of maggots

IT WAS estimated that the UK bait market for anglers, including maggots, was worth somewhere between £25 and £30 million per year in 2024. A large portion of this consisted of worms and maggots; maggot sales are estimated at 1,000 tonnes of bait annually.

Big roach on fly

ANOTHER FINE roach meriting special mention is one of 3lb 9¾oz taken in June, 1949, by Mr T. G. Player, from the Thames at Sonning; and two particularly intriguing roach in the records of rod-caught three-pounders are a specimen of 3lb 8oz captured by Mr W. Morfitt in September, 1935, from a pond at Kilpin, Howden, Yorkshire (just imagine it, a pond three-pounder!), and one of 3lb 4 oz caught by Mrs W. Fennell on the Test with a mayfly on May 27, 1929.

Faddist, *Roach Fishing*, 1953

Spectral fishes

Within the streams, Pausanias saith,
That down Cocytus valley flow,
Girdling the grey domain of Death,
The spectral fishes come and go;
The ghosts of trout fly to and fro,
Persephone, fulfil my wish,
And grant that in the shades below
My ghost may land the ghosts of fish!

Andrew Lang, *Angling Sketches*, 1891

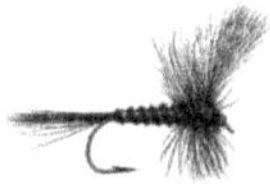

'Very subtil'

THE CARP … a very subtil fish, and hard to be caught.

Izaak Walton, *The Compleat Angler*, 1653

✵

The perch … prince of the prickly cohort.

Decimus Magnus Ausonius

✵

A perch of 4lb 15oz was caught on a worm on the Thames at Chertsey in September 1941 by Mr F. Steel of Putney.

Insects for chub

MY FRIEND dropped one or two of his insects down, and presently one of the largest chub I ever saw came out from cover; it was quite seven pounds in weight, and looked in magnificent condition.

The postman was on his mettle, because I was an interested spectator; he alternated his hooked beetle with loose ones; but the one that had a hook in it was severely left alone. At last, on my whispered suggestion, when the fish refused it, he lifted it from the water and dropped it behind him close to his tail. I don't think I ever saw a chub take a bait quicker; he wheeled round in a moment, and had it like a flash.

The rest of the adventure can be described in a few words.

The chub made a headlong rush into the jungle of weeds below, and half the tackle only came back the next moment; the water was ridged as though a steam plough had been driven beneath it. My friend said he had never calculated the cost, and how it would have been possible to land it from such a place, where … he was up a tree, some seven or eight feet above the water.

J. W. Martin, *My Fishing Days and Ways*, 1906

✵

Chub … fearfullest of fishes.

Izaak Walton, *The Compleat Angler*, 1653

First-ever mention

Who has not seen the scarus rise,
Decoyed, and killed by fraudful flies?

Martial, *Epigrams*

Mad bleak

THE BLEAK is of the carp species, and, in shape, a handsome formed fish, with a bright green back, and brilliant silvery scales on the sides, and has a fine large eye, altogether much like a fresh-caught sprat: they spawn about the middle of March, but sooner recover themselves than any other fish. The bleak is not much prized at table, from their small size, and tasting somewhat bitter, which happens, however, only in the Summer months. In Spring and Autumn, many persons who like small fish fried, think the bleak well tasted, and prefer them to roach or dace. In Summer, bleak are sometimes much distressed by an insect called a hair worm; they then swim on the surface of the water, being unable to descend; and when in such condition, they are called, by fishermen, Mad bleak.

Edward Jesse, *An Angler's Rambles*, 1836

Different worms used by anglers

Lobworms – those big worms you see on your lawn late at night in wet weather. Much loved by chub, barbel and other big fish anglers.

Dendrobaenas – a small to medium earthworm much loved by bream anglers (mostly). A compost worm but especially good at breaking down tougher brown material – sticks and so on.

Mealworms – not really worms at all but rather the larval form of the yellow mealworm beetle. Difficult to put on the hook and they have a tendency to float when thrown in as loose bait but some anglers swear by them, especially for winter chub.

Bloodworms – again not a real worm but the larval form of many different chironomid flies. You need very, very, small hooks for these, but match fishermen often use them with great success.

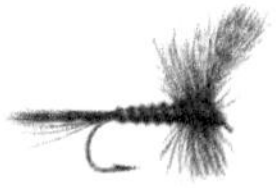

Brandling or red worm – smaller than the lobworm and they live only in manure heaps. They have a curious ability to exude a pungent odour when threatened – no doubt an adaptation designed to put off any bird or other predator trying to eat them.

For sea anglers, lugworm and ragworm are an absolute must.

The blow lugworm or sandworm, grows to about 13cm and lives entirely under sand on most British beaches where its casts can usually be seen.

Black lugworm grow even bigger. Ragworm, like lugworm, spend their lives under sand. They belong to a group of more than 500 different species so far identified. They have strong teeth – and they bite!

✵

And if ye angler take fysshe; surely thenne is there noo man merier than he is in his spyryte.

Juliana Berners, *Treatyse of Fysshynge Wyth an Angle*, 1496

✵

> While others fish with craft for great opinion, I with great truth catch mere simplicity.
>
> Shakespeare, *Troilus and Cressida*

Figwort trout

HE SPED past me, and got to grips with the plant *Scrophulariaceae aquatica*. Figwort as I have said, is a noble plant; and if inflexible tenacity counts for anything in the plant world it must be noble indeed. My fly, an

olive, had played maypole round those hideous figwort spikes dodging in and out among the tiers of claret whorls in a manner wonderful to behold.

It was then that I began to doubt the wisdom of Providence in placing this noble plant on the edge of a trout stream. Even old Gerarde considered it much overrated, censuring those 'who doe rashly teach that it kept a man in health'. After a time, I managed to rescue the olive, a little dishevelled and the gut about its head somewhat frayed. The spike of figwort had also suffered, but of that I took no heed.

The fish were now rising in a manner joyous to behold. A fat monster not ten yards from me was feeding like a provincial alderman. I dared not risk that frayed cast, so, hastily extracting a new fly from my box, I bit through the gut – and stuck the fly firmly in my thumb. The delay was maddening, but at last I was ready and cast once more well upstream.

This time the wind carried my fly straight on to an old post sticking out of the river. Time to give up.

P. B. M. Allan, *Trout Heresy*, 1936

The Mexican blind cave fish lives in the dark and has completely lost the use of its eyes.

Brown trout and sea trout are the same species but some migrate to sea while others stay at home.

Cleverer than trout

THE BARBEL would not need such a liberal handicap as you imagine. Pound for pound, he is a much more powerful fish than a trout.

Cholmondeley-Pennell remarks that barbules appear to be given, as a valuable equivalent, to species which, restricted by instinct

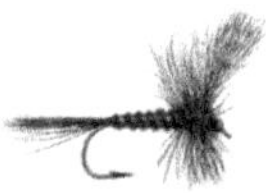

to feeding near the bottom of water that is often turbid and deep, must necessarily experience more or less imperfect vision from the deficiency of light.

Yet the sight of the barbel is not only as keen as that of the trout but, I will venture to say, even keener. Time and again I have been amazed at the distance at which barbel in shallow water can detect one's presence, and no barbel that I have ever seen will eat when it is wittingly in the presence of mankind, however far off the intruder may be. And, by the way, they feed on the bottom, not near the bottom. Their eyes, also, can move more freely in the socket than can those of trout.

I have already stated my belief that the barbel is higher in the scale of fish intelligence than the trout.

H. T. Sheringham, *An Open Creel*, 1910

Arm'd cap-à-pie with baskets, bags and rods,
The angler early to the river plods:
At night his looks the woeful truth announce,
The luggage half a ton, the fish – an ounce.

Quoted in Arthur Ransome, *Mainly About Fishing*, 1959

Ugh, chub!

THE LOGGERHEADED chub, is called by the French *un vilain*, because he is not good for the table.

Francis Francis, *A Book on Angling*, 1867

Chapter 3

WEIGHTY MATTERS

Melancholy

> I'll tell thee more of this another time, but fish not with this melancholy bait, for this fool's gudgeon, this opinion.
>
> Shakespeare, *Hamlet*

✵

In a single spawning the ocean sunfish (*Mola mola*) lays an incredible 300 million eggs!

Fish rubbing

INSTEAD OF taking a large fish to a taxidermist as British anglers have traditionally done, Japanese fishermen keep a record of a particularly good fish by rubbing one side of the fish with a special ink and then pressing rice paper down on the fish to leave a scale-perfect portrait. It's an art form known as *gyotaku*.

Most polluted

THE RIVERS Mersey and the Nant both in northern England are among the most polluted rivers in the UK. The Mersey suffers from sewage pollution, the Nant from heavy metal pollution, particularly lead, zinc and cadmium. But the Mersey is improving and flounders are now found in the estuary. Freshwater fish upstream including perch, chub and even barbel are also reported. The Nant, a tributary of the Tyne, is also slowly improving.

Salmon stocking

EFFORTS TO restock the Thames with salmon have been relatively unsuccessful. Thousands of fry released in the 1970s produced a good number of returnees in the years that followed but numbers have since declined. Ten tagged hatchery fish captured in 2003 and sixteen returning untagged adult salmon captured between 2005 and 2008 were all salmon that had simply returned to the wrong river. Genetic tests showed they were fish born in other rivers in southern England, which just goes to show that the salmon's homing instinct is by no means infallible.

Hagfish and lampreys

HAGFISH AND lampreys are unique because they are the only living representatives of jawless vertebrates (agnathans), providing insights into the evolution of early vertebrates and their body plan.

Hagfish, which famously produce vast amounts of slime when threatened, have a skull but no vertebral column – this is unique among living creatures today.

They are among the most primitive fish in the world and have been around for at least 100 million years.

Only goers

LONDON MATCH-FISHERS until the 1980s had a curious rule – that only what were called 'goers' could be weighed in at the end of the day.

So, gudgeon for example, had to be 5in long, roach 8in, dace 7in, chub 11in and so on. Anything smaller could not be weighed in. Pike and eels were also inadmissible.

The system, to which many anglers would like to return, meant that smaller fish – more vulnerable to stress – were returned immediately to the water rather than being kept in a keepnet until the end of the day. When the system was abandoned, everything could suddenly be weighed in which meant matches were often won with hundreds of tiny bleak or other small species.

The divine gudgeon

THE LENGTH of the *Cyprinus gobio* (the humble gudgeon) seldom exceeds eight inches. Both its size and plumpness are correctly are praised by [the Roman poet] Ausonius and Ovid speaks of its smooth spineless back, as contrasted with the bristling spines of the perch, which frequents the same localities. Mere urchins, eat, and angle for gudgeons … to enjoy which Ptolemy invited over to Egypt, Archephon, from Attica; this bon-vivant went, and was offered there at supper a portion of a small dish of these delicacies, which he let pass without taking any. Conduct so strange and unexpected made Ptolemy first stare, and then mutter to his confidant that he must have invited either a blind or an insane man to his table. Whereupon Alcanor good-naturedly put the guest's abstinence in a new and more favourable light, by attributing it entirely to modesty: 'He saw it, sire, but deemed himself unworthy to lay profane hands upon so divine a little fish.'

Charles Badham, *Fish Tattle*, 1854

Huge trout of Loch Awe

THE READER of Mr Colquhoun's delightful old book, 'The Moor and the Loch', must not expect Loch Awe to be what it once was. The railway, which has made the north side of the lake so ugly, has brought the district within easy reach of Glasgow and of Edinburgh. Villas are built on many a beautiful height; here couples come for their honeymoon, here whole argosies of boats are anchored off the coasts, here do steam launches ply. The hotels are extremely comfortable, the boatmen are excellent boatmen, good fishers, and capital company. All this is pleasant, but all this attracts multitudes of anglers, and it is not in nature that sport should be what it once was. Of the famous *Salmo ferox* I cannot speak from experience. The huge courageous fish is still at home in Loch Awe, but now he sees a hundred baits, natural and artificial, where he saw one in Mr Colquhoun's time. The truly contemplative man may still sit in the stern of the boat, with two rods out, and possess his soul in patience, as if he were fishing for tarpon in Florida.

Andrew Lang, *Angling Sketches*, 1891

Longest migration

THE DORADO catfish has the longest freshwater migration of any fish species – it starts life in the upper Amazon River and then drifts down to the estuary for a few years before making its way back again. A total journey of perhaps 10,000 miles.

Trouting Eden

A Mr Roberts from Carlisle was fishing the River Eden in Cumbria when he hooked a trout. Now most of the Eden's trout at this time weighed just a few ounces and there were so many of them that it was difficult to get through to anything bigger. Most fishermen were therefore happy to accept that a big bag of little fish was the most they could expect. However, as soon as he hooked this particular fish, Mr Roberts knew that he'd achieved the impossible. He'd hooked a big trout and from the feel of the thing it probably weighed nearer two pounds than one. Terrified that it might get off he played it with the utmost care. He led it gently up and down the river and silently prayed each time it leapt and somersaulted in its efforts to get free. But at last it began to tire and he drew it across the water to the waiting net.

At that precise moment a massive bird of prey – Mr Roberts later claimed it must have been an osprey or an eagle – swooped down and along the river, talons dragging viciously below it. The bird hit the fish at about thirty miles an hour and scooped it into the air to the utter astonishment of Mr Roberts. The eagle – if that was what it was – soared into the sky. Mr Robert's best ever trout from the Eden dangled beneath it. Mr Roberts, normally a sober, churchgoing man, let out a series of terrible oaths. Line was shooting away off his reel as the bird steered a course toward the distant hills. Mr Roberts took up the slack line, but the instant the bird found itself being tugged in the wrong direction, it let go of the trout. The trout fell into the middle of the river, but when Mr Roberts reeled in, he found that the best trout he'd ever hooked in the Eden was just a mangled wreck.

Newcastle Chronicle, 1862

> Lie thou there, for here comes the trout, that must be caught with tickling.
>
> Shakespeare, *Twelfth Night*

Jock Scott

THE JOCK Scott, one of the oldest salmon flies, incorporates twenty-two different fly-tying materials – everything from Indian crow to blue macaw, mallard, feathers, jungle cock and swan.

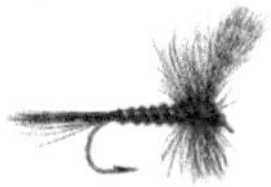

Walking anglerfish

THE AUSTRALIAN anglerfish, is unique in that it uses pelvic and pectoral fins to walk on the ocean floor instead of swimming.

✵

Among the world's smallest artificial flies are aphids tied on size 22 and 24 hooks – little more than a millimetre or two long.

✵

More than half a million lakes and ponds have been destroyed and filled in or built over in the UK in the century to 2024.

✵

The deepest lake in the UK is Loch Morar in Scotland at 310m – deeper than London's Shard is tall!

✵

The biggest carp ever landed on rod and line weighed more than 112lb.

✵

The fish species most caught in the UK is the mackerel.

✵

The smallest of Britain's officially listed record rod-caught fish is the common goby – the current record weight is just 1g.

✵

Other tiny rod-caught records include the three-spined stickleback at just 8mg. Light rod fishers (LRF) specifically target tiny species including the boar fish, butter fish and dragonet.

Clarissa

THE MOST famous record-breaking fish ever caught in Britain is Richard Walker's record carp, Clarissa, caught from the legendary Redmire Pool in Herefordshire in 1952 and weighing 44lb. The fish spent the rest of its life – more than thirty years – as a hugely popular attraction in London Zoo.

Thin lipped

THE FORMER British record boat-caught thin-lipped mullet was landed in Christchurch Harbour in 1981 by Tom Quinn. It now sits in the Natural History Museum store, next to many of Charles Darwin's specimens collected during the voyage of HMS *Beagle*. The fish weighed 2lb 9oz and 8 drams. The record was broken a little later the same year by six-year-old Ian Williams fishing in exactly the same spot.

More clever carp

MR JESSE says of some Carp and Tench which were kept by him, that 'they were soon reconciled to their situation, and ate boiled potatoes in considerable quantities; and the former seemed to have lost their original shyness, eating in his presence without any scruple'. My experience agrees with Mr Jesse's. I have now three sturdy little fellows, in a vivarium within a few yards of me, that will readily take anything I throw them, and almost out of my fingers.

These fish have been in the house for nearly a year, and are apparently doing well and growing.

One of them affords a good instance of the 'hard-dying' qualities of the species. He was 'killed' in the usual manner, and consigned, with others, to the cook, in whose care, however, after some hours, he began to show signs of revival. A kind-hearted damsel compassionately transferred him to the vivarium, where he has since thriven, showing no effects of his narrow escape, save a scar on the back of the head, which he will probably never lose.

There is a pretty instance on record of the taming of the Carp by a little American girl. The child, who was not six years old, lived close to the bank of a pond in the village of Rocky Nook, near Kingham, Massachusetts. She began by throwing crumbs into the water.

Gradually the fish learned to distinguish her footsteps, and darted to the edge whenever she approached; and at last, they would even feed out of her hand, and allow her to stroke their scaly sides. The control of Van Amburgh over his wild beasts was not more complete than that which this child attained over her finny playmates, who rejected all overtures from the rest of the neighbours, and would have nothing to do with any but their tried friend.

They would trust no one else, let him come with food ever so tempting; and when a few years afterwards the child unfortunately died, during a visitation of cholera, the fish are said to have shown the most marked symptoms of distress, swimming disconsolately up and down at the spot where their protector was wont to look for them, and refusing the food offered by the good-natured townsfolk. 'Thus,' as the writer adds, 'it will be seen that even fishes are not so cold-blooded but that they will recognize the law of kindness'.

At Sir J. Bowyer's, near Uxbridge, Mr Bradley tells us, there is a pond full of tame Pike which can be called together at pleasure. Mr Salter was acquainted with a person who for several years kept, in a water-butt, a Perch, which came to the surface for his food whenever his owner tapped on the side of the butt. According to ancient sources some fish species could be lured to their destruction by the sound of castanets.

Professor Rennie states that in Germany fish are still taken by nets hung with rows of little bells arranged so as to chime in harmony; and, without going back to the story of Amphion and the Dolphins, or the old Scottish Harper who, according to the ballad, 'harp's a fish out o' the salt water', we may find hundreds of well authenticated anecdotes, leading clearly to the conclusion that fish have a very considerable perception of external sounds.

A rather annoying proof of the acute hearing at least of the Carp species is nightly furnished me by the three individuals in my vivarium, already referred to. Every evening, when the bell is rung for family prayers, these fish commence springing and splashing about in the water, continuing their efforts for five or ten minutes with a noise and vivacity exceedingly distracting to the attention, and in the highest degree indecorous.

The Carp was a well-known fish in the times of the ancient Greeks and Romans, though apparently held in no very high estimation. It is mentioned by Aristotle and Pliny, the former naming it Kuprin's, or Kapranos, from whence probably originated the Latin term Cyprinus, and also the modern appellations Karp (Swedish), Karpf (German), Carp, Karpe, and Carpe (English, Danish, and French), Carpal (Spanish), and Carpione (Italian).

When, and whence, the Carp was first brought into this country – if indeed it was really an introduced fish at all – is involved in obscurity. Leonard Mascall, a gentleman of Sussex, claims to have been the importer both of the Carp and of the Pippin; but Mascall's time was 1600, while numerous notices of the Carp appear nearly a century before that date. The old couplet quoted by Izaak Walton:

Hops and turkeys, carps and beer,
Came into England all in a year –

appears also to have been written under a poetic licence.

H. Cholmondeley-Pennell, *The Angler Naturalist*, 1875

Heraldic tench

IN HERALDRY, the tench has not been made so much use of as many much poorer, and not less common fish: the old German family, Von Tanques, bears in their arms three, or [gold]; three tench haurient [as if rising for air], gules, are the arms of the French family Tanche: a Flanders marshal carries the same; and Sir Fisher Tench has adopted his namesake as part of his coat of arms.

Charles Badham, *Fish Tattle*, 1936

Better than gold

THE ANCIENTS knew nothing of procuring pearls from bleak scales, but they certainly had an equivalent; for Chares of Mytilene speaks of a fish in the Indian seas, oblong in shape, like a pearl oyster, and of an agreeable smell, whose bones (called perri) furnished ornaments for the ear, and arm and ankle rings; and was more prized – and paid for – by the Medes, Persians, and Asiatics generally, than even solid weighty gold itself.

The Angler's Notebook and Naturalist's Record, 1880

Sole of discretion

SOLES ARE distinguished from plaice by having no tubercles on the skin; from halibuts by the smallness of their teeth, which are confined to one jaw; from turbot, by their eyes lying on the right in place of the left of the mouth (which is also twisted to one side), and by the comparative shortness of the dorsal fin. They have a very wide range, extending southward from the Scandinavian and Baltic seas, along the Spanish and Portuguese coasts into the Mediterranean; they are a frequent fish in America; an excellent kind abounds at the Cape of Good Hope; and, not to mention other foreign sites, constitute, as all the world knows, one of the commonest as well as best productions of the British seas, swarming along most of our sandy shores.

Though sea-fish by birth and by rights, they will not only live, but thrive in fresh water, and like it so well, as sometimes of their own accord to ascend rivers to a considerable height, and nestle for months in slime at the bottom, where they grow apace; indeed, when some have been retained in fresh, and others of a light weight placed in salt water, the first, after a year's sojourn, have been known to grow faster than their salty cousins.

The Angler's Notebook and Naturalist's Record, 1880

Lady of Babylon

THAT MOST cunning of all fish, the carp, may be taken in this way when it would be hopeless to fish for him with the bait hanging

just off the bottom, for he could then see the gut at once, and also the shots that weight the line, and probably the float above; and if the float is of a nice white and vermilion, or some other dazzling rainbow colour, it will afford the old carp a capital text on which to preach an instructive sermon to the young ones on scarlet abominations and the Lady of Babylon.

Francis Francis, *A Book on Angling*, 1867

Perch weights

ARLESEY BOMBS are weights designed to fish Arlesey Lake in Hertfordshire. They were designed by Richard Walker, later famous for catching the biggest carp ever landed in Britain. He needed something he could cast long distances into the deepest part of the lake – perhaps 50ft deep – where the biggest perch lived. The weights were streamlined which also helped stop them snagging in weed. Using these weights Walker caught a 4lb 13oz perch in the early 1950s which held the British record for some time.

In an appalling act of vandalism much of Arlesey Lake was destroyed by developers – it was partly filled in and the site used for landfill. A small part of the lake was still there in 2024 but the owners no longer allowed fishing.

Tyne record

THE RECORD sea trout from the Tyne, as of 2025, weighed 17lb 4oz. It was caught by twelve-year-old Adam Haughton from Haltwhistle.

Test record

THE BIGGEST sea trout from the Test weighed 28lb 5oz and was caught in 1992.

Thames records

THE BIGGEST chub ever caught from the Thames – as of 2025 – weighed 9lb 3oz and was caught in 2012.

The biggest dace ever caught from the Thames weighed 1lb 3oz. It was caught in 1964.

The biggest-ever Thames gudgeon weighed 4oz 8 drams.

Gudgeon fascination

FEW FISH bite more eagerly than gudgeons, and this perhaps is the reason why so many persons may be seen patiently sitting in punts from morning to night on the river Thames employed in catching these fresh water smelts. There appears indeed to be a fascination in gudgeon fishing which it is not easy to account for; and the wonder is increased when we see three or four persons in a punt lightly jerking a rod every instant, and watching a float as it glides down the stream before them, the sun sometimes scorching them, and at others the rain wetting them through.

Edward Jesse, *An Angler's Rambles*, 1836

Wily old fellow

A WORM or other bait only just touching the bottom, with a row of shot 6in or 8in above it, is very likely to challenge the attention of the carp, who at once sees something he is not accustomed to, and becomes suspicious.

To show how different it is when the line rests on the bottom, I once took a 7lb carp on an eel line with a coarse string snood and worm bait. Carp always nibble a good deal at the bait before they take it, and will often nibble off the tail of the worm, or suck off your paste and leave the hook showing without taking the hook at all. In using paste I prefer sweet paste, made up with honey or brown sugar, to plain, and I have heard of paste made of pound cake being greatly affected by the carp.

Poor old Bill Kemp, now with the majority, a capital old carp fisher at Teddington, used to put on a lump of this as big as a large gooseberry, and fish it with ledger tackle; and he used to take a great many fine carp. He was a wily old fellow, and many a good day's sport

I had with him in days gone by, but poor old Bill went the way of all flesh, though he left many good fishermen of his own name behind him, who still keep up their calling at Teddington.

Francis Francis, *A Book on Angling*, 1867

✵

A float is pleasing in appearance and even more pleasing in disappearance.

H. T. Sheringham, *An Open Creel*, 1910

Ancient groundbait

IT IS curious that this groundbaiting should have been practised more than sixteen hundred years ago; it is described by Oppian [the second century Greco-Roman poet] who says that the paste was made with scented cheese and flour, which was divided into little pellets and scattered in by the fisherman to attract the fish.

A singular expedient for catching Carp is suggested by Mr Fitzgibbon in his Notes to Walton. 'A correspondent,' he says, 'not long since wrote to me for advice. He had a pond in which were many large Carp; and although he had angled for them in due season from February to October during seven years, he had not succeeded in capturing them. I advised him to line with hurdles the bank of the pond at the spots where he meant to fish – to groundbait those spots with red worms, gentles, and especially with sweet paste, for three or four days – to then take his rod, and, supporting it on a bifurcated prop (cut off the branch of a tree) inserted in the bank behind the hurdles, to place on his line a hook broken off at the bend, that is, without barb or sharp point – to bait this harmless hook with sweet paste, and to sink it nearly to the bottom of the already ground-baited water.

The Carp will soon take this bait; and finding they can do so with impunity; they will become bolder hourly. Replacing the bait every time it is nibbled off, and continuing to do so for three or four days, commence then angling in earnest: with the same rod and line, but with a barbed hook baited exactly as before, come behind the hurdle, and, with very

light float, angle cautiously. My correspondent acted on my advice, and succeeded in catching as many of the large Carp as he wanted.

The Angler's Notebook and Naturalist's Record, 1880

Giant roach

IN THE early 1930s, the editor of *The Angler's News* for his annual big fish lists had to raise the minimum weight for eligible roach from 2lb to 2lb 4oz. This notwithstanding, the number of roach included in the list for the 1934–35 season was seventy-nine, and rose to eighty-nine in 1935–36!

Ageing fish

OTOLITHS – A calcium carbonate structure in the inner ear (commonly known as ear stones) – exist in the inner ear of all vertebrates. Concentric rings on the otolith can be counted and provide a precise measure of the age of a fish.

Bristling perch

I HAVE, when pike-fishing in a lake or river, seen a large perch sail with prickly fin erect close up to the boat or bank, seize the pike bait, and shake it as a terrier does a rat, eventually getting the head and hook into his mouth, bristling all the while like a porcupine, and his colours showing with increased brilliancy; then, retiring, with his prey, only to be hooked and caught himself.

Alfred Jardine, *Pike and Perch*, 1905

Pike sex

QUESTION OF Determination of Sex. I notice that you have accepted the statement as to the presence of milt and absence of roe in the 37½lb Avon pike (the Record fish) as proof that the fish was a male and I – again with trepidation – venture to suggest the possibility of the observer having mistaken fat for milt.

Very little, if any, spawn would be showing in this fish at the date it was caught, October, and, while in all probability there would be quite 1lb of fat adhering to the gut of an Avon pike of this weight, this fat looks very much like the milt of a male fish. I opened a pike of $21\frac{1}{4}$lb which was taken from the Avon on December 5, 1944, and weighed the fat I took out ($\frac{3}{4}$lb); the ova had just started to form and there was enough to show me the fish was a female.

The largest male pike I have ever handled over a period of 45 years was 16lb and looking back now in the light of mature experience I consider that even in that instance I may have mistaken the fat for the milt of a male. I was not quite so observant then as now and the interest in the question of sex was not so marked.

Letter from fish taxidermists Coopers, to *The Angler's News*, December 1944

Ocean records

THE PACIFIC Ocean yields 70 per cent of the world's wild caught fish total catch. The Atlantic comes second followed by the Indian Ocean.

Rarest fish in the UK?

THE VENDACE is the rarest freshwater fish in Britain, found only in Derwentwater in England's Lake District. A 2008 survey found that a Bassenthwaite Lake population was extinct. Scotland once had two vendace populations – in Mill Loch and Castle Loch – but both are now extinct.

Spey casting

A DAY'S fishing on the River Spey at a time of year when you have only a small chance of catching a salmon might cost as little as £50; for a day at the best time of year you might pay at least £500. Even £500 does not guarantee you a fish, however.

What's my line?

MONOFILAMENT LINE – used by almost every angler. It's cheap, stretches (but not too much!) and used with the correct knots is reliable. But it does wear out easily and is almost too cheap – anglers are often accused of discarding it unthinkingly leaving it to damage wildlife and the environment.

Fluorocarbon line is more expensive and less reliable than monofilament but has better abrasion resistance (it's harder for a fighting fish to cut the line by running through weed or rocks), but it is less reliable. Its great advantage is that it is virtually invisible under water.

Braided line is thinner pound for pound than either monofil or fluorocarbon and it has no stretch so bites are instantly detected. The downside is that without stretch it is vulnerable to breakage – a lunge from a hard-fighting fish will often break the line.

Fishing line strength to line diameter

0.06mm	12oz
0.07mm	1lb 2oz
0.08mm	1lb 12oz
0.09mm	2lb
0.10mm	2lb 6oz
0.12mm	2lb 14oz
0.12mm	3lb 4oz
0.14mm	4lb 12oz
0.16mm	5lb 10oz
0.18mm	6lb 8oz
0.20mm	7lb 12oz
0.22mm	9lb
0.24mm	10lb 4oz
0.26mm	11lb 6oz

Traditional targets

DESPITE NOT being hard fighters nor growing to especially large sizes, roach have always been one of the most popular fish among anglers. Partly this is down to their strikingly beautiful appearance – bright silver with equally bright red fins, but also because the rarity of large roach traditionally made a target fish of 2lb-plus the fish of a lifetime.

For bream anglers a target fish of 10lb was always the thing to aim at; or a 20lb carp or a 5lb chub. Increasingly sophisticated hi-tech tackle and rigs (poly bags, hair rigs and electronic bite alarms) have made these target sizes seem small to many anglers, but traditional anglers remain happy to catch the traditional target sizes using methods that give the fish a better chance of coming out on top.

Confessions

ONE OF the most popular fishing books ever written is *Confessions of a Carp Fisher* by Denys Watkins-Pitchford, better known as BB. The author acknowledges that he has never caught even a moderately big carp but the appeal of the book lies in his masterful evocation of the magic of carp and carp fishing.

Casting record

THE WORLD-RECORD longest beach cast in the UK, as of 2025, was a 150g lead cast an astonishing 281.75m (308yd).

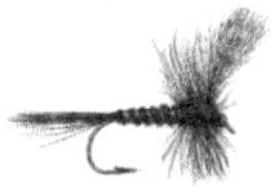

Moving barbel

BARBEL, ONE of the most loved fish among UK anglers, occur naturally in eastern-flowing rivers such as the Thames but – surprisingly – they did not exist in the River Severn or the Trent until the 1950s when they were artificially introduced. Rivers that have been stocked with Thames barbel include the Stour, Bristol Avon, the Teme and the Great Ouse.

Distance travelled

AN ATLANTIC salmon may travel more than 4,000 miles in its lifetime. That's around 1,200–1,800 miles from UK rivers to its feeding grounds off Greenland and the Azores and then the same distance back again. A very small number of salmon may make the journey twice – so as much as 8,000 miles over a lifetime.

Tiny shark

THE DWARF lanternfish is the world's smallest shark – adults reach just 7in long. They live at depths of up to 2,500ft.

Canon's fly

THE GREENWELL'S Glory was first tied in the late 1890s by James Wright. Wright had been asked by the churchman Canon Greenwell, after whom the fly is named, to imitate real flies – olives – on the Tweed. The Greenwell's Glory is still one of the most popular and successful flies ever invented.

No definite article

FROM THE late nineteenth until the late twentieth century, newspapers and magazines referring to 'the River Tweed' in terms of fishing, never used the definite article. The correct form was 'I was fishing on Tweed' not 'I was fishing on the Tweed'. No one knows where the tradition began or why it eventually vanished.

Marine discoveries

ROUGHLY 2,000 new marine species – that includes fish, crustaceans, corals and much more – are discovered each year.

Women anglers

ESTIMATES GIVE the number of women anglers in the UK as varying from less than 1 per cent of all anglers to not more than 10 per cent.

Eating the seed corn

EUROPEAN EEL numbers have dropped by 95 per cent as of 2025 according to best estimates. The decline, as always with threatened species, is down to human activity – pollution, dams, over-fishing, hydroelectric power schemes and, of course, global warming. Extraordinarily, the catching of glass (baby) eels – immature youngsters – is still permitted in some places despite the fact that this is effectively like eating seed corn. Killing glass eels means killing millions of eels before they have a chance to reproduce.

Sea angling statistics

RESEARCH IN 2023 suggested that more than half a million UK adults had been sea angling in the previous year. Their total catch was estimated at around 7 million fish retained and 28 million fish released.

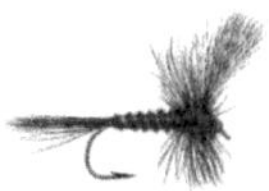

Crayfish nightmare

AMERICAN SIGNAL crayfish look like small freshwater lobsters. They also taste very similar to them. In the 1970s the government allowed imported crayfish to be bred commercially for food, thinking this would be a good way to provide a livelihood for any number of crayfish farmers.

The market for crayfish was disappointing and, whether by accident or design, a few signal crayfish escaped. Fifty years later, the Thames and the Kennet to name just two rivers, are slowly being destroyed by millions of signal crayfish. Crayfish will eat anything and everything which means coarse fish eggs now have far less chance of producing new generations of fish. The white-clawed native crayfish, which is unable to compete with the signal, is now almost extinct in the UK.

Jellyfish soaring

JELLYFISH NUMBERS have soared in many areas of the world's oceans largely because humans have caught or killed many of the species that naturally feed on jellyfish, such as swordfish and tuna. Jellyfish numbers were formerly kept in check because they had to compete for food with, for example, anchovies, but so many anchovies are now caught each year that there is far more food for the jellyfish.

A fish, not a horse

THE SEA horse is actually a fish and, incredibly, there are more than forty separate species. None is recorded as having ever been caught by an angler!

Sea horses have segmented armoured plates that slide over each other to allow the sea horse to remain flexible. Species range from 1.5 to 35cm (0.6 to 13.8in) and they are found all over the world – from the Thames Estuary to the Pacific Ocean.

Lateral thinking

A FISH may not have ears but it has a lateral line – a long line of highly sensitive cells running down each of its sides. The line can detect everything from heavy footfalls of a clumsy bank angler to temperature and water pressure.

Brains

THE BRAIN of fishes, which is exceedingly small in proportion to their size, is formed by an enlargement of the extremity of the nervous axis, or spinal marrow, and is disposed as in reptiles, with the addition of 'nodes' or 'ganglions' at the base of the nerves of smell. The proportionate weight of brain in a Pike, as compared with its body, is 1 to 1300; in the Shark, 1 to 2500; and in the Tunny – a remarkably stupid fish – 1 to 3700.

The Angler's Notebook and Naturalist's Record, 1880

Women on top

THE BIGGEST game fish caught on rod and line in the UK was landed in 1922 by Georgina Ballantine. It was a 64lb salmon from the River Tay. Her record has never been beaten.

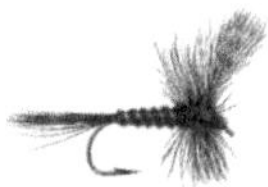

Four million eggs

THE PRODUCTIVENESS of fish – a productiveness compared to which that of every other living creature appears insignificant – is limitless as the seas through which they are destined to range. The young produced by one Cod-fish at a single deposit have been found to number little short of four million, and those of a Flounder to exceed one hundred and forty thousand.

The Angler's Notebook and Naturalist's Record, 1880

Clever carp

OF ANY species with which we are acquainted, carp are one of the easiest to tame. They feed readily in stews, and will come for their meals, according to some authors, at the ringing of a bell – certainly at the sound of their keeper's voice. Mr Bradley, who was a great observer of the habits of fish, relates an instance of this: 'At Rotterdam, in a garden belonging to M. Eden, I had the pleasure of seeing some Carps fed, which were kept in a moat of considerable extent. The occasion of my seeing these creatures was chiefly to satisfy me that they were capable of hearing.

'The gentleman having filled his pocket with spinach-seed, conducted me to the side of the moat. We remained quiet for some time, the better to convince me that the fish would not come till he called them. At length he called in his usual way, and immediately the fish gathered from all parts of the moat in such numbers that there was hardly room for them to lie by one another.'

The same sort of thing may be witnessed in the waters of some public gardens near Rotterdam. In these ponds the Carp are also in the habit of following visitors about, in expectation of food; and one immense fellow, with a side as broad as a flitch of bacon, and an appetite that seemed insatiable, actually pursued me for nearly a hundred yards along the side of the bank, until, my stock of bread being exhausted, I was fain to try experiments with some paper pellets, when he sailed off in magnificent disgust. This fish must have weighed, I should think, at least 15lb.

H. Cholmondeley-Pennell, *The Angler Naturalist*, 1875

One thing is admitted ...

SOME 150 years or so ago carp fetched a higher price than salmon.

Francis Francis, *A Book on Angling*, 1867

Chapter 4

COOKING UP A STORM

Cat's barbel

WITNESS THE constant practice of those numerous anglers who grab each liquid foot of Thames from Putney Bridge to Twickenham ... when (as sometimes happens even to the clumsiest) they haul a noble barbel from the water, having, with a view both to immortalize themselves and encourage others, weighed, registered, and frescoed his full-length portrait on the walls of the inn, they then give up the noble carcase to the landlord's cat, to divide with her feline friends as she pleases.

Charles Badham, *Fish Tattle*, 1854

Rascal

Enjoy thy stream, O harmless fish,
And when an angler for his dish,
Through gluttony's foul sin,
Attempts – a wretch – to pull thee out,

God give thee strength, O gentle trout,
To pull the rascal in!
John Wolcot 'Peter Pindar' (1738–1819), *The Ballad of a Fish in a Brook*

Salmon skin leather

AN IRISH company perfected a means to turn salmon skin into fish leather which was made and marketed throughout the 1980s and 1990s. It was made into dog collars, wallets, even shoes. It was just like the finest leather made from cattle but never seemed to quite shake off its fishy smell!

Anglerfish

NUMEROUS SPECIES of anglerfish famously have what are effectively fishing rods sticking out of their heads. On the end of these protuberances are tiny fleshy 'lures'. The anglerfish waves its fishing rod and lure until a smaller fish investigates. When the small fish gets near enough the anglerfish pounces. Even more bizarrely, many species of anglerfish reproduce by absorbing the male into the body of the female.

Queen's cane

QUEEN ELIZABETH the Queen Mother (1900–2002) refused to use salmon rods made from modern materials. She used an 18ft cane rod that shocked several of her gillies who could barely lift the rod themselves.

Somersaults for food

AUTHOR AND angler Denys Watkins-Pitchford, better known as BB, caught a large carp, took it home to his garden in Northamptonshire,

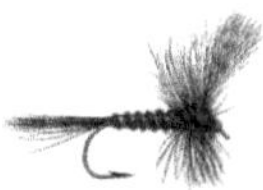

and released it into his pond. Over the years that followed he taught it to jump somersaults in return for food offerings.

Tom Quinn, *BB Remembered*, 2006

High among the finny tribe

GALEN [the ancient Greek physician] speaks in no measured terms of the excellence of the gudgeon, declaring it to rank very high amongst the finny tribe; not for the mere pleasure of eating it, but for the satisfaction attending its easy digestion. The moderns coincide with the ancients respecting the wholesomeness of this fish, though it is now never seen at a dinner-party, unless, perhaps, at some Thames-side villa, where still, in imitation of Pope:

> Although no turbots dignify rich boards,
> Are gudgeons, flounders, what the Thames affords.

Charles Badham, *Fish Tattle*, 1854

Mother cod

THE BIGGEST cod ever recorded (not caught on rod and line) weighed an extraordinary 96kg (211lb 10oz). It was 1.8m long.

✵

The biggest fish ever caught on a fly rod was a 600lb mako shark caught off the coast of California in 2009.

✵

> Your bait of falsehood takes this carp of truth.

Shakespeare, *Hamlet*

✵

> I am stung like a Tench.

Shakespeare, *Henry IV, Part I*

Worthless bream?

THE BREAM is as worthless a fish as the mendole [the tiny blotched picarel], but without compromising the taste or reputation of him who eats it.

It has even found partisans. As Chaucer writes:

Full many a fair partrich had hee in mewe,
And many a *brome*, and many a luce [pike] in stewe,

Izaak Walton also speaks well of it; Cuvier concedes it to be a moderately good fish; but his countrymen, going beyond him, have this proverb, 'Who has bream in the pond may ask friends to his table.'

Charles Badham, *Fish Tattle*, 1854

On the breeding of pike

ON THE breeding of pike, Walton informs us that it occurs once a year, in the following manner: A he and a she usually go together out of a river into some ditch or creek, and then the spawner casts her eggs, and the milter hovers over her all the time she is casting her spawn, but touches her not.

The spawning season occupies from two to three months; the young pikesses of three years taking the lead, and when they have been all safely delivered, the dowagers, or frog pikes (so called from their period of spawning being late, with the frogs), succeed them.

The Angler's Notebook and Naturalist's Record, 1880

Salmon naming game

IN THOSE modern countries where salmon abounds, it is usual to designate it, as Ausonius [the Roman poet] has done, by a variety of names according to its age: this is the case in Germany, and also in some parts of England: thus Willoughby tells us that of salars

caught in the Ribble, those of the first year are called smolts; those of the second year, sprods; those of the third, trouts; those of the fourth, fox-tails; those of the fifth, half-fish; and only after that period, salmon.

It is not improbable that Ausonius may have mistaken, under the names salar and fario, different species of fish, as, till quite lately, the parr which abounds in some Scotch rivers, and notably in the Clyde, was erroneously supposed to be juvenile salmon; indeed the similarity in the markings of many species of young trout still makes it very difficult to say of a given specimen whether it will turn to a grilse, a young bullhead, a salmon trout, a river trout, or a true parr.

William Jardine, *British Salmonidae*, 1841

Record pearls

A NINE-YEAR-OLD boy fishing for trout at Tweed Mill, Coldstream in 1886, caught a mussel 4in long and 2in broad, containing no less than forty fine pearls of different sizes. He earned more for this one catch than his father, a farm worker, had earned in the previous five years.

Trout – no tails or eyes

AN ACCOUNT of some tailless trout having been discovered in a loch on Islay. Although surrounded by other lochs in none of them were tailless trout found save in it, and there they were in excellent condition.

At the mines of Wanlochhead, Dumfriesshire and Leadhills, in Lanarkshire, there are, according to Dr Grierson of Thornhill, streams coming from the shafts, in which trout without tails, and often deficient in fins, are frequently caught. Such fish are often blind.

Whitaker's Almanack, 1871

Male mothers

THE SEA horse – remarkably – relies on a curious reproduction system. After the female lays her eggs in the male's pouch, he keeps them alive until they have grown sufficiently and then gives birth to live young.

All males

ALL AUSTRALIAN barramundi start life as males and then at three or perhaps four years of age they undergo a metamorphosis that turns them into females. They are exceptionally hard-fighting fish and have been widely stocked for that reason.

Kitchen fish

CHINESE FAMILIES in rural areas traditionally kept a few fish in carefully made channels – rather like wide, open pipes – through which the waste water from their kitchens ran. Scraps would be thrown into the water after meals and during washing up – as the food was washed away it would be eaten by the fish waiting in the channels. When the fish were big enough, they would be eaten by the family!

Weed control

GRASS CARP from the Far East were introduced to the UK as a method of weed control – they live almost exclusively on weed and can clear a lake in no time. But like many if not most introduced species their arrival had unforeseen consequences.

For a start they will eat *all* the weed in a waterway, which isn't necessarily a good thing. They also out-compete native fish. However, they do have less of a damaging impact than many other introduced species for the simple reason that they cannot naturally reproduce in most of the countries, especially in the northern hemisphere, to which they have been introduced.

Grass carp can grow to be almost 7ft long and can weigh as much as 100lb. They are popular among anglers but have one major drawback – with their almost purely vegetarian diet they are very difficult to catch!

Climbing eels

IT WILL be remembered by those who have read that most delightful of angling books, *My Life as an Angler* (1876), that Mr Henderson mentions the annual ascent of the rocky barrier, some sixty feet in height, which forms the Newton Don waterfall on the river Eden, not far from its junction with the Tweed, by vast multitudes of small eels, about four inches in length.

These eels are bred in the brackish tidal waters of the Tweed and in their endeavours to reach the upper pools of the Eden and its tributaries, have to scale the heights of Newton Don, which they accomplish by wriggling and clinging to the wet moss.

There was a time no doubt when eels had not learned to make this ascent, but the thoughts of eels as of men, are 'widened by the process of the suns'.

It is stated that the Falls of Trollhättan on the Wenern [Vänern], in Sweden, formed an impassible barrier to the eels in their progress from the sea until about fifty years ago, and that they now attain the upper water of that river where none were formerly to be found. Another note may also be made on eels.

The Scotch detest them. The peasantry regard them as a species of water serpent. 'I well remember,' says Mr Henderson, 'giving my good old landlady, Mrs Johnston, some eels to cook for dinner, and her remonstrations: "Nay, nay, Mr Henderson, surely ye wudna hae me touch thae serpent beasts. Think now o' what the serpent did to poor Eve; nay, aw canna get ower that."'

This dislike is widespread. The Red Sea fishermen regard eels with great aversion. Every individual met with is condemned to death. They are never eaten.

The Angler's Notebook and Naturalist's Record, 1880

Rents for fishing

RENTS FOR fishing have soared. This is, of course, partly due to the low value of sterling, but also to the fact that there are now so many more fishermen. About 65 years ago my grandfather paid £25 for fishing for the season. That same fishing, which is not nearly so good now, lets for £275. The motor car has proved to be a two-edged tool. It enables us to get to out-of-the-way places only to find other people there who would probably not have walked or bicycled, as we might have done.

G. P. R. Balfour-Kinnear, *Angling* magazine, January 1959

Wickerwork

FROM THE 17th century until well into the 20th century anglers often carried a creel – a wickerwork basket, curved to fit the side of the body and suspended from a shoulder strap. Tin models were tried as well as expensive and beautiful embossed leather models, some of which survive. Most of these creels were pot-bellied and the wicker examples were frequently fitted with a slot in the lid through which any fish could be dropped. The origins of the word creel are obscure but it is probably derived ultimately from the Latin *craticular* meaning a lattice-work or barred structure.

Angling magazine, June 1956

Difficult with the dry fly

FOR SOME reason the Tweed is more difficult to fish with the dry fly than the Test, for example. The water is swifter and very dark, it drowns the fly soon, and on the surface the fly is less easily distinguished than at Whitchurch, in the pellucid streams.

The Leader, a tributary, may be fished with dry fly; on the Tweed one can hardly manage it. There is a plan by which rising trout may be taken – namely, by baiting with a small red worm and casting as in fly

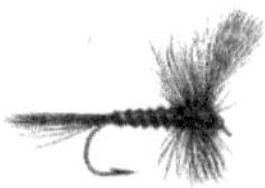

fishing. But that is so hard on the worm! Probably he who can catch trout with fly on the Tweed between Melrose and Holy Lee can catch them anywhere.

On a good day in April great baskets are still made in preserved parts of the Tweed, but, if they are made in open water, it must be, I fancy, with worm, or with the 'screw', the larva of the Mayfly.

The screw is a hideous and venomous-looking animal, which is fixed on a particular kind of tackle, and cast up stream with a short line. The heaviest trout are fond of it, but it can only be used at a season when either school or university keeps one far from what old Frank, Walton's contemporary, a Cromwellian trooper, calls 'the glittering and resolute streams of Tweed'.

Difficult as it is, that river is so beautiful and alluring that it scarcely needs the attractions of sport. The steep banks, beautifully wooded, and in spring one mass of primroses, are crowned here and there with ruined Border towers – like Elibank, the houses of Muckle Mou'ed Meg; or with fair baronial houses like Fernilea. Meg made a bad exchange when she left Elibank with the salmon pool at its foot for bleak Harden, frowning over the narrow 'den' where Harden kept the plundered cattle.

Andrew Lang, *Angling Sketches*, 1891

Wary

The wary luce [pike], midst wrack and rushes hid,
The scourge and terror of the scaly brood.

Ausonius, 'Moselle', *c.* 371 AD

Barbel stocking

IN SEPTEMBER 1896 a consignment of 100 Thames barbel, captured at Staines by Mr Gomm was placed in the Stour at Iford Bridge. All the barbel in that river descend from these fish and Stour specimens of 14lb are regularly landed.

Perfect and good

Would'st thou catch fish?
Then here's thy wish;
Take this receipt
To anoint thy bait.
Thou that desirest to fish with line and hook,
Be it in poole, in river, or in brook,
To blisse thy bait, and make the fish to bite,
Loe here's a means if thou canst hit it right;
Take gum of life, fine beat and laid to soak
In oyle, well drawn from that which kills the oak;
Fish where thou wilt, thou shalt have sport thy fill,
When twenty fail, thou shalt be sure to kill.
It's perfect and good
If well understood
Else not to be told
For silver or gold.

John Dennys, *The Secrets of Angling*, 1613

The Odyssey

EVEN, AS when a fisher on some headland lets down with a long rod his baits for a snare to the little fishes below, casting into the deep the horn of an ox of the homestead, and as he catches each flings it writhing, so were they (the companions of Odysseus) borne upward to the cliff (by Scylla).

Homer, *Odyssey*, Book XII

... and The Iliad

AS WHEN a man sits on a jutting rock and drags a sacred fish from the sea with line and glittering hook of bronze, so on the bright spear dragged he Thestor.

Homer, *Iliad*, Book XVI, *c.* 750 BC

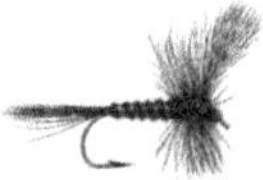

Tackle tip from 1810 when all lines were silk or horsehair

THE ROTTING of the line is not always to be provided against. It will happen now and then. Take boiled oil and gold size (some prefer copal), a wine glass of the first to a dessert spoon of the second, steep well, rub off all surplus, and dry as quickly as you can.

Thomas Salter, *The Art of Angling*, 1833

Wild brown from the Thames

LARGE WILD brown trout are rare in the River Thames but an angler fishing at Windsor just below the Victorian railway bridge in the Home Park managed it. But the trout was hooked in a very unusual way. The angler was testing a new pike lure – a jointed plug more than 6in long. He'd cast and retrieved the lure several times when on the next retrieve he felt a huge thump and the rod bent into a hoop as a big fish bored downstream.

Convinced he had hooked a salmon the angler played the fish carefully for the next ten minutes. At last, the fish began to tire and came to the surface a few feet from the bank. The 'huge' salmon turned out to be a 3lb trout but hooked through the top of its tail fin! Foul-hooked fish always fight harder but with its movements barely restricted by the tail-hook hold, this trout had fought like a fish ten times as big.

Ugliest?

ONCE DUBBED the world's ugliest animal for its soft, lumpy appearance, the blobfish was crowned Fish of the Year by a New Zealand environmental group in 2025. The annual competition, held by the Mountain to Sea Conservation Trust, aims to raise awareness of New Zealand's freshwater and marine life.

The blobfish isn't actually as shapeless as it looks when caught. It lives at immense depths where water pressure squeezes it into a more normal shape. Other fish that have won this bizarre competition include the orange roughy, a fish with mucous canals on its head. The roughy is a member of the delightfully named slimehead family.

Painting an angling fanatic

ONE OF the best known and most amusing angling pictures of the nineteenth century is Theodore Lane's *The Enthusiast*. The picture, now in the Tate Gallery, was first exhibited in 1828 and although it gently pokes fun at the angling fanatic it is undoubtedly a good indication that by the early years of the nineteenth century, angling was already being seen as an obsessive sport, or perhaps more accurately a sport pursued by obsessives.

Most fishermen will know exactly how the enthusiast in the picture felt as, forced to stay at home with an injured (or gouty foot) he set up his tackle and fished in a tub of water in his sitting room.

Lane, who was born in London in 1800 and studied as a print colourer, died tragically early. He fell through a skylight in a house in the Gray's Inn Road in London and was killed instantly. He was just twenty-eight. *The Enthusiast* was copied by numerous other artists throughout the nineteenth century.

The angling comedy

THE COMIC, or at least more light-hearted aspects of angling, still attracted a number of late Victorian and Edwardian painters like Walter Dendy Sadler (1854–1923). Sadler is a particularly good example, and though he was not well known as an angler he painted a number of interesting and highly amusing pictures. His *Pegged Down Fishing Match* is a wonderful satire on the superficial absurdities of match fishing, where anglers line out along the bank at 30-yard intervals to catch as many fish as they can, only to throw them back at the end of the day.

Sadler's other angling pictures include one of the most reproduced of all angling images: his *Thursday – Monks Fishing* has been used on countless postcards and prints. He also painted *It's Always the Largest Fish that's Lost* (1881), *A Goodly Catch* (1884) and *Gudgeon Fishing* (1885).

Sadler was adept at painting coarse as opposed to game fishermen and he went to some pains to emphasise what he obviously saw as their static, rather dogged attitude to their sport. Not for the coarse fisherman the pleasures of wandering the riverbank looking for a rising fish. Instead, the coarse fisherman is portrayed by Sadler in a way that indicates he is addicted to the slow, seemingly endless task of sitting still in one position on the riverbank.

Sadler's *On the Way To Fish* is something of a departure from this formula. Painted in 1880, it shows a wary, portly angler gazing suspiciously out from the canvas as he makes his way along the riverbank. The intention of the picture, as with all Dendy Sadler's work, is to portray the angler as a harmless, but rather comic figure – a view with which many anglers would agree.

✵

A fishing rod is a stick with a hook at one end and a fool at the other.
James Boswell, *The Life of Samuel Johnson*, 1791

✵

The American definition of an angler:
A jerk at one end of the line waiting for a jerk at the other end.

Dead sheep

FOR THOSE with their own fishing it was once common to hang a dead sheep (or goat, dog or even cat) from a branch above the river. Maggots would develop on the carcase and fall continually into the river below. After a couple of weeks, fish would be queueing up in the river a little downstream of the suspended sheep making the angler's job a great deal easier. Victorian records suggest that as many as one hundred barbel might be caught in a single sitting as a result.

Gozzers, pinkies and jokers

THE UK'S favourite fishing bait – the humble maggot – was once more commonly known as the gentle.

Maggots come in an extraordinary range – from jokers (the larvae of the gnat) to pinkies (greenfly larvae), squats (housefly larvae), gozzers (bluebottle larvae). So effective are maggots that their pupal stage – known as casters – are also very useful.

Risky bait

A RISKY bait once very popular was the wasp grub. To get a bucketful you need to break up a wasps' nest without getting stung in order to collect the wasp larvae, which look like giant maggots.

Weird but successful ...

COARSE FISHING baits include prawns, potatoes, luncheon meat, sweetcorn, chocolate, chilli-flavoured bread, wheat, hempseed, cow's brains, cheese, old bacon, elderberries, silkweed, popcorn, halibut and other pellets, worms of every conceivable type, dog food, slugs, crayfish, sweetcorn, peanuts, and a great deal more!

Eel puzzle solved

SCIENTISTS HAVE long been puzzled by the European eel's habit of travelling thousands of miles to the Sargasso Sea to breed. Why go so far? The answer, it seems, is that when the European and American continents were much closer to each other the journey was far shorter, but as the continents drifted apart over tens of millions of years, the eels kept to their ancestral journeyings despite the gradually increasing distance.

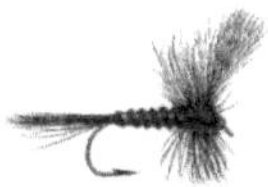

Sighing for the pike rod

IT SEEMS worthy of note that the 'purist' as a rule is a man who has served a long apprenticeship at other kinds of fishing before finally giving himself up to the dry fly, which argues that after much experience of fishes and methods of catching them he has come to the conclusion that the greatest amount of tranquil pleasure is to be got out of the use of the dry fly.

But it is largely a personal matter. I know several expert dry-fly men who prefer roach fishing, others who are happier with their cast of three flies whipping some northern burn, and yet others who in the midst of the Mayfly season may be heard sighing for autumn and the pike rod.

The Angler's Notebook and Naturalist's Record, 1880

The cod's revenge

THE STUPIDITY of commercial fishing can be judged by the history of the Grand Banks off the coast of Newfoundland.

For decades in the middle and late twentieth century, millions of tonnes of cod were taken by increasingly vast trawlers from this extraordinarily rich area of the sea. Factory ships grew ever bigger to catch more of the fish and those who operated the fishery believed – contrary to all common sense – that however many fish were taken, the Grand Banks would always provide more fish.

By the late 1980s the fishery had totally collapsed and it has still not recovered despite a ban on fishing. Numerous communities along the seaboard were devastated by the closure of the fishery.

In 1968, 810,000 tonnes of cod were caught but even as the catch declined each year thereafter nothing was done. In one fifteen-year period, 8 million tonnes of cod were caught. Still nothing was done. In 1991 the catch had plummeted to 129,000 tonnes and in the following year the fishery was closed: around 37,000 people lost their jobs as a result. Decades of mismanagement going back to the 1950s was the cause of the collapse and the fishery had still not recovered by 2025.

By 1993 it was estimated that just 1 per cent of the historic numbers of northern cod were left.

Local fishermen blamed factory ships from Eastern Europe as well as government secrecy about what was really going on. Some say it will take a century for the fishery to recover because the almost total destruction of the cod stocks led to a vast increase in other species including capelin. Capelin had been a main source of food for the cod in earlier times, but the species now dominated the Grand Banks and larger capelin devastate the juvenile cod.

The Grand Banks has the dubious claim to be the most stupidly managed fishery in the world.

Virgin birth

HAMMERHEAD SHARK and zebra shark have both been recorded as producing young through a process known as parthenogenesis otherwise known as virgin birth. Where males are scarce, these sharks are able to produce eggs that develop into shark pups without the need for male sperm.

Hook don't play

BARBEL FISHING was only rarely indulged in by landowners and aristocrats (in the UK often one and the same thing), but the barbel's reputation as a sporting fish meant that they would occasionally head down to the river.

As aristocrats were very rarely able to do anything on their own, they would employ a servant to bait a particular spot with tens of thousands of lobworms for several days before fishing was planned to take place.

On the appointed day the aristocrat would be handed a rod with a bunch of worms and a weight attached. He would cast into the spot where all those lobworms had been deposited and then he would do something very odd. As soon as he had hooked a fish – and after days of pre-baiting the river would often be alive with barbel – he would

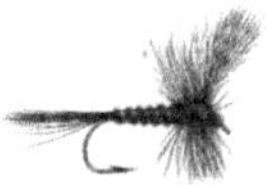

immediately hand the rod to his servant to play and land the fish. Hooking the fish was seen as the skilled part whereas playing the fish was seen as being beneath the dignity of the nobly born.

Carp growth

IN OPTIMUM conditions – a warm lake with plenty of food – carp can reach weights of 20lb in just two years.

Cucumber

THE SMELT is said to smell like cucumber while the grayling smells so distinctly of thyme that it takes its Latin name from the plant – *Thymallus*.

Deepest dive

THE DEEPEST a shark has ever been officially recorded is 3,700m – that's more than 12,000ft! The record-holding Portuguese dogfish is found across many of the world's oceans – from the Atlantic to the Mediterranean – and reaches a maximum length of 3ft. It is a member of the group of sharks known as sleepers – which famously includes the longest-living vertebrate, the Greenland shark.

Purists at Redmire

PURIST ANGLERS no longer use electronic bite alarms or carbon rods preferring instead to use centrepin reels and cane rods. Casting any distance with a centrepin reel is very difficult whereas a complete novice can cast long distances with a fixed spool reel.

Proving that older techniques can work well, the doyen of traditional anglers, Chris Yates, broke Richard Walker's decades-old carp record (just over 44lb and caught in the early 1950s) using a centrepin reel and a cane rod. Indeed, Yates caught his fish (51lb 5oz in 1980) from Redmire Pool in Herefordshire – exactly the same place where Walker caught his record fish.

Electric but not eels

DESPITE THEIR name, electric eels are far more closely related to catfish than to eels. In fact, they are knifefish, a large group of animals in the genus *Electrophorus*. Weirdly they must surface regularly to breathe air. They are found in South American freshwater particularly in the Amazon and its tributaries.

Electric eels produce enough electricity to kill a human – more than 800 volts in one shot. The electricity is produced in modified muscles known as electrocytes – these are very much like cells in a battery. Electric eels grow throughout their lives continually adding new vertebrae!

Drying the fly

ONE MORE convenience is a small tobacco tin containing a small piece of flannel on which has been smeared a teaspoonful of the Mishustin [line grease] mentioned before. This is for greasing the line, a thing that may have to be done two or three times a day. The flannel is best carried in a tin, so that the greasing process may not involuntarily be extended to other property. Further, the little oil bottle should have a piece of string tied round its neck by which it can be slung to a coat button, or, better, to the landing-net sling.

And, finally, the question of boots and the probable state of the river banks should have been considered. If the fishery to be visited is boggy or sloppy on the banks, or if the meadows adjoining it are ‘under water’, that is to say, are being irrigated by the drains from the river (it is often a question of the time of year) the novice would do well to take his waders. If he does not possess then let him invest.

The possession of a tin of line-greasing stuff bought at the tackle maker’s renders the tobacco tin unnecessary. Each shop tin contains a bit of stuff for applying the grease. Amadou, which I have

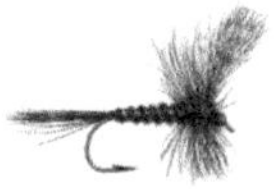

mentioned earlier, is nowadays an essential thing for the dry-fly man, and I always carry a piece, using it for drying the flies as well as the line.

Squeeze a sodden fly in it and it will come out quite dry, though it may want 'preening'. Amadou can be got at a chemist.

The Angler's Notebook and Naturalist's Record, 1880

Spotting the kelts

BY THE way, the novice may be enjoying these sensations in spring or early summer, in which case let him beware of the kelt, or spent salmon, lest, having killed it, he finds himself sitting in a far less exalted position, for the kelt is protected by law.

The ordinary kelt, blotched and hideous, will not bother him; even the partially mended kelt, for all its silver, is so big of head and shrunken of flank that it is easily detected. But the 'well-mended' kelt is the dickens, the more so because there is, apparently, a kind of degenerate salmon which potters about estuaries instead of going honestly to sea, and then ascends rivers in a half-fed condition, technically clean (since it has been in salt water), but practically nothing of the kind.

The only certain method that I know of to convict a well-mended kelt is to examine its vent carefully. Some signs of past inflammation are sure to be visible; if so, the fish is a kelt, and to be returned, for the vent of the clean fish is small and free from any trace of inflammation. But it is not so very long since I made up my mind from this and other external indications that a certain fish was a kelt and another angler of far greater experience confirmed my view.

A post-mortem examination and the presence of fairly well-developed roe proved it to be a clean fish.

I wish the novice luck.

The Angler's Notebook and Naturalist's Record, 1880

Salmon questions

1. Why is it that on one day salmon are scared right out of a pool by the mere sight of a prawn, or even by the smallest shrimp, when, on the following day (while, so far as we can see, conditions are similar) every fish that sees a prawn will take it greedily?
2. Why will salmon take a spinning bait readily every day for a week or more and then, when there has not been any change in the water or the weather, refuse it for several days but take a fly instead?
3. When trout are feeding on nymphs, say 10 inches under the surface, why will they refuse a nymph that is, perhaps 3 inches or perhaps 18 inches deep?

Although I have been fishing for so many years, I regret to say that I am not able to answer any of these questions.

G. P. R. Balfour-Kinnear, *Angling* magazine, May 1960

No egg-aggeration

THE CARP is extraordinarily prolific – so much so that the roe of a single female, if allowed to arrive at maturity, would be an ample stock for many acres of water. In a fish of 9lb weight Bloch found 600,000 eggs, and Schneider 700,000 in one of 10lb weight.

Even these numbers, however, astonishing as they are, sink into insignificance when compared with those of the ova of the Sturgeon. In the Volga, where this fish grows to from 13 to 16 feet long 200lb of roe have been taken from one specimen, which, at the rate given by Pallas, viz. five eggs to the grain, would make a total of 7,000,000.

From one of these Volga Sturgeon, captured in the winter of 1769 and measuring 17 feet, 720lb of roe were taken, containing on the same calculation 25,200,000 eggs.

This account, however, applies only to Sturgeon of Northern waters, for M. Petit found less than 1,500,000 ova in a large specimen from the south of Europe. The same gentleman counted 60,000 eggs in a Smelt, 350,000 in a Tench, 50,000 in a Roach, 6000 in a Shrimp, from 12,000 to 21,000 in a Lobster, 4000 in a Crab, 36,000 in a Herring,

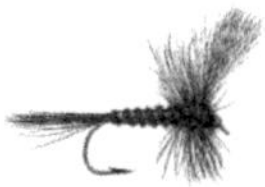

9,000,000 in a Cod, 1,500,000 in a Mackerel, 1,000,000 in a Sole, and the same number in a large Flounder. Even the liquor of the Oyster contains incredible multitudes of small embryos.

H. Cholmondeley-Pennell, *The Angler Naturalist*, 1875

Monastic

THE MONKS, who particularly cultivated the carp at many of their monasteries, had regular succession ponds for breeding and feeding them; clear pure water, and plenty of it, running over a sweet gravel bottom being the last stage they went through before being tabled – bread and milk and other farinaceous diet being used to fatten and sweeten them.

Francis Francis, *A Book on Angling*, 1867

Chapter 5

ON THE PROWL

Fishing foxes

ROACH FISHERMEN on the tidal Thames were disappointed as the river became cleaner through the 1960s and 1970s. Their favourite quarry reduced in numbers and the lower river began to be dominated by large shoals of sometimes very large bream.

In the summer at Kew and Chiswick, the bream can often be seen breaching in the shallows when the weather is particularly warm and on numerous occasions reports have circulated among anglers that foxes have been seen dashing into the water to grab a large bream for dinner.

Longest-living vertebrate

USING RADIOCARBON dating of the proteins in Greenland shark eyes, scientists have confirmed that large specimens may be 500–600 years old, making them the longest-living vertebrates on the planet. Weighing up to 2,200lb and reaching lengths of 21ft and more they are also one of the world's largest sharks.

Slow moving and living at great depths in the North Atlantic and Arctic oceans, (around 1,000m) they are also one of the least-understood species of fish on the planet.

What we do know is fascinating, however. The Greenland shark, for example, has the slowest swim speed of any fish and the slowest tail beat. How it still manages to be an effective predator is something of a mystery. One answer is that they must mostly scavenge – remains of moose, bears and other land mammals have been found in Greenland shark stomachs.

Fishing for Skeggers on the Thames

[SALMON PARR or skeggers were once fished for on the Thames at Laleham.]

The river is very narrow and shallow in this part and on these shallows many Fish are taken by whipping, particularly a delicious Fish called the Skegger, supposed to be of the Salmon species.

You whip for them with a fly-rod, light line, and No. 10 hook, baited with a gentle; a red-palmer is also a good bait. These Fish are allowed to be caught during the fence-months, on the principle that they are going to leave the river, probably never to return, as the time of their migration is during the fence-months.

In the Summer, Chub and Dace are taken here in the same way of angling, substituting a fly for the gentle.

Thomas Salter, *The Art of Angling*, 1833

Sweet eels and tench

IN ONE day we caught about twenty brace of extraordinary carpes, with very sweet eels and tench; I believe I shall hardly forget the pearch of eighteen inches long … nor the old gentleman's resolution; while we were drinking a dram of the bottle, a fish run away with his rod which he being unwilling to loose, stript off his cloathes and leapt in, securing at last both rod and fish triumphant.

John Whitney, *The Genteel Recreation*, 1700

Dead cat

The best gentils [maggots] I know, breed from a dead cat.

John Whitney, *The Genteel Recreation*, 1700

Hale old water fox

COUNTLESS, INDEED, are the sites, both at home and abroad, where some sly old cyprian attains a Nestorian longevity: almost every piece of water maintains some such traditional patriarch. Not long ago one of these hale old water-foxes was to be seen, in a parallelogram college-pond at Cambridge University, who still continued to champ the green duckweed with a smack, and to flounder heavily amongst the startled water-lilies, on his veteran flank, as he used to do in our pupillary days, some twenty years back. He has seen out many a generation of bed-makers and ten-year men. The Lodge has had many a new cook, since he first swam there; yet, amidst all these culinary changes, no one has been permitted to lay fraudulent hands upon him; his safety is supposed to be identified with the interests of the college; and thus protected by common consent from hook and every harm.

Charles Badham, *Fish Tattle*, 1854

Eat no fish

DERCETO [a Syrian fertility goddess known for having a woman's face and a fish's body] by the wiles of Aphrodite fell in love with a beautiful young man and was brought to bed of a daughter: being ashamed of what she had done, she slew the young man, exposed in the desert the child (who, fed with milk and then with cheese by pilfering pigeons, grew up to become the famous Semiramis) and then cast herself into the lake at Ascalon and was transformed into a fish – whence it came to pass that at this very day the Syrians eat no fishes, but adore them as gods.

Ovid, *Metamorphoses, c.* AD 8

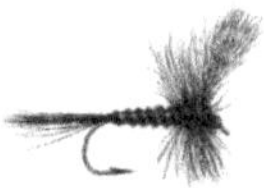

Travelling barbel

RESEARCH AT the University of Bournemouth in 2022 suggested some fascinating facts about barbel. There were two studies of twenty fish tracked for two years. Remarkably some fish travelled great distances – up to 12km up and then down their rivers, while others tended to stay in the same areas. It was these latter fish that tended to be caught more often by anglers.

Trouting from the weir

THE ART of fishing for trout from the tops of the weirs of the river Thames, is, I may venture to say, confined to very few, and to those only who have been in the habit of practising it for a considerable length of time. It requires good tackle, great skill, and some nerve. A bungler would even find it difficult to put a bleak properly on a set of the hooks which are used in Thames trout fishing, so as to make it spin as it ought to do.

The angler sits or stands on the top of the piles of the weir, the foaming water rushing through them with great force and noise.

The torrent then forms eddies, and little whirlpools in the basin below, and from which as the water expands itself, it again resumes its calm and stately movement. In the position I have described, the angler has to cast his line into the foaming basin, and this a skilful practitioner will do to a distance of from thirty to forty yards. The great art, however, is in gathering up the line properly in the hand for a second cast, so that it may not become entangled, or be checked in its progress.

When the position of the angler is considered, this is no easy task, especially as the loss of his balance might precipitate him into the torrent below. I do not mean to say that all Thames trout are taken by anglers while in this position, as some persons troll from boats or the banks of an ait, but the best, and generally the most successful fishing, is from the tops of the weirs.

Edward Jesse, *An Angler's Rambles*, 1836

Big carp are very seldom caught in winter … and that goes for spring, summer and autumn.

Phantom, *The Angler's News*, 1950

Servants

THE LONDON angler does not require a servant to carry his fish and landing net, or to wade the water, to land a fish, but trusts to his own dexterity.

John Baddeley, *The London Angler's Book or Waltonian Chronicle*, 1834

Leg for bait

THERE IS one well-attested story of a pike attacking a human. It happened on a lake near Hazlemere in Surrey in 1881. A newspaper reported that a boy swimming saw a pike lunge up out of the water and sink its teeth into his leg. The boy scrambled out of the water with the pike still attached!

Cat caught the pigeon

CATFISH ON the Tarn river that runs through the town of Albi in southern France have learned to attack and eat pigeons that come to the water's edge to drink and bathe. The catfish have been so successful at this that many have reached more than 10ft in length.

Both fish died

TWO 20lb-plus pike were found dead in a trout lake in Kent – the bigger of the two had tried to eat the slightly smaller fish which had become stuck in the bigger fish's throat. Pike teeth point down towards the gullet so the bigger fish could neither eject the smaller pike nor swallow it so both fish died.

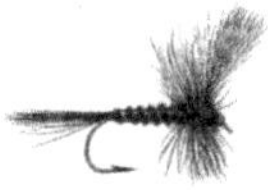

✵

The great Izaak Walton never spoke of 'anglers and very honest men' but of 'anglers or very honest men'.

Death of a favourite lamprey

MUCH WILL be found on the Roman custom of keeping tame fish, chiefly from Varro and Pliny. The latter tells us that a functionary, called the 'nomenclator', was maintained, who gave the fish their particular names and taught them to 'wag their tails, fawn like dogs, and permit themselves to be scratched and clawed'. Extraordinary attachments were formed. Hortensius, the orator, nearly broke his heart on the death of a favourite lamprey.

Many of the Conscript fathers [the senators of ancient Rome] … and other eminent personages were so much under fish fascination that they thought no time or trouble too great if they could but train some docile favourite to feed out of their hand; and that object once attained, they were rapt in an Elysium of delight. Cicero called two of his friends subject to this delusion 'Tritones piscinarum', tritons of fish-ponds; and 'Piscinarii, or stock-pond men'.

The pastime of feeding fish was not confined to the ancient Romans, for it obtains among various tribes of modern people. Mr Ellis writes, 'Fish are great favourites in Otaheite, and are fed in large holes half-filled with water. I have been frequently with a young chieftain when he has sat down by the side of a hole, and, giving a whistle, has brought out an enormous eel, which has moved about the surface of the water, and eaten with confidence from his master's hand.'

The Angler's Notebook and Naturalist's Record, 1880

Freezing surgeon

ROACH AND dace fishers form another distinct class of Thames fishermen, and it is very seldom they try for anything else, or indeed, understand any other sort of fishing. So keen, however, are they at this sport, that many pursue it very late in the year; and a retired surgeon, of the name of Wood, is still talked of at Hampton, as having braved the coldest weather in winter in order to follow his favourite diversion. He would get up before it was light, have his breakfast, and fish till it was dark, at a time when the wet was freezing on his line. He had always, however, a hot dinner brought to the boat, which must have kept him from starving.

Edward Jesse, *An Angler's Rambles*, 1836

Crystal streams

All in the fragrant time of day,
E'er Phoebus spreads around his beams,
The early angler takes his way,
To verdant banks of crystal streams.

Richard Brooks, *The Art of Angling*, 1766

With patient skill.
Attending to the trembling quill.

John Dennys, *The Secrets of Angling*, 1613

✵

The great Denys Watkins-Pitchford, author of the *Confessions of a Carp Fisher*, which was published to acclaim in 1950, insisted that, 'Carp fishers disappear in autumn and are not seen until the following midsummer, nobody knows where they go or what they do.'

Jardine's pike

FISHING IN the 1890s, Alfred Jardine caught five pike weighing a total of 172lb. The smallest of these pike weighed 30lb 8oz; the largest 37lb.

Thames sturgeon

STURGEON OCCASIONALLY come up the Thames, but they were never numerous in this river. Provision was made in

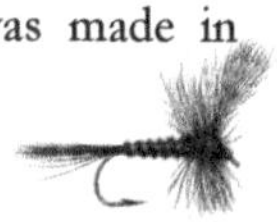

ancient Acts excepting them from the vulgar fate of other fish, and in the instructions to the City water-bailiffs for the time being, orders were issued that the sturgeon 'was not to be secreted', and that all royal fishes taken within the jurisdiction of the Lord Mayor of London, as namely, whales, sturgeons, porpoises, and such like, should be made known, and the name and names of all such persons as shall take them shall be sent in to the Lord Mayor of London for the time being.

The sturgeon therefore is always, when taken, sent direct to grace the table of majesty.

Charles Dickens, *A Dictionary of the Thames*, 1851

Pike attack

A PIKE is said to have attacked the foot of a Polish damsel – a performance the more ungallant as the ladies of Poland are celebrated for their pretty ankles.

There are various accounts of the assaults of Pike upon the legs of men wading; and the author has himself had the privilege of being severely bitten above the knee by a fine Thames fish, which sprang off the ground after it was supposed to be dead, and seized him by the thigh, where it hung, sinking its teeth deeply into a stick which was used to force open its jaws.

Bentley's Miscellany, 1851

Many great pikes

ONE OF my name was the best Trouler, for a Pike, in this Realme: he laid a wager, that he would take a Pike of four foot long, of Fish, within the space of one Moneth, with his Trouling-Rod; so he Trouled three weeks and odde days, and took many great Pikes, nigh the length, but did not reach the full length, till within the space of three dayes of the time; then he took one, and won the wager.

Thomas Barker, *The Art of Angling*, 1651

Neat osier pannier

YOUR PANNIER cannot be too light; I have seen some made of osiers, cleft into slender long splinters, and so wrought up, which is very neat, and exceeding light: you must ever carry with you store of hooks, lines, hair, silk, thread, lead, links, corks of all sizes, lest you should lose or break, as is usual, any of them, and be forced to leave your sport in quest of supplies.

Robert Venables, *The Experienced Angler*, 1662

Scalded lines

APART FROM fish, fishing in New Zealand is full of incident and interest. The animals and plants belong not only to another hemisphere, but, it may be said, to the prehistoric past. Geologically there are strange things to be seen. A geyser which shoots off every three hours prevented me one evening from fishing a very excellent pool. Where boiling streams enter cool rivers, care must be taken that gut and line are not scalded.

J. C. Mottram, *Fly Fishing: Some New Arts and Mysteries*, 1914

Of worms for anglers

Cleanse them from filth, to give a tempting gloss.
Cherish the sullied reptile with damp moss;
Amid the verdant bed they twine, they toil,
And from their bodies wipe their native soil.

John Gay (1685–1732), author of *The Beggar's Opera*

On Rods, Lines, Gut, Hair, and Hooks

AS THE angle-rod is a material article in the Angler's Catalogue, great care should be taken to procure a good one. The fishing-tackle shops keep a great variety, made of bamboo, cane, hazel, hickory, &c., and of different

lengths; some fitted as walking-canes, and others to pack in canvas bags; the latter are to be preferred, because you may have them of any length, and they are made more true, and are stronger; the rods made to pass for walking canes seldom exceed twelve feet, which is, generally speaking, too short; those made of bamboo-cane are best for general fishing, having several tops of various strengths; but the rods made of the white cane are much superior for fine fishing, particularly for Roach, being very light in weight, yet stiff.

In choosing a rod, observe that it is perfectly straight when all the joints are put together, and that it gradually tapers from the butt to the top, and is eighteen feet long; if longer, they seldom play true. Some strong and fit for trolling; others for Barbel, Perch, &c.; all of which should have rings on every joint, and some finer for Roach, &c.

Thomas Salter, *The Art of Angling*, 1833

✵

When the wind is in the east, the fish bite least. When the wind is from the west, the fish bite best.

English proverb

✵

Without effort you won't even pull a fish out of a pond.

Russian proverb

✵

Frateretto calls me and tells me Nero is an angler in the lake of darkness. Pray, innocent, and beware the foul fiend.

Shakespeare, *King Lear*

Angling writer and illustrator

UNIQUELY AMONG angling writers, Denys Watkins-Pitchford (who wrote under the pseudonym BB) also illustrated his books. Typically, those not in the know would buy a copy of one of his books and read that the author was BB and the illustrator Denys Watkins-Pitchford, thinking them two different people. BB illustrated more than thirty of his own books and as many as sixty books by other writers. He is perhaps best known not for his fishing books but for his children's books including the Carnegie Medal-winning *Little Grey Men*.

Famous rod

THE MOST famous fishing rod in England is not as one might have imagined a hi-tech, super-efficient carbon rod. In fact, it's the Richard Walker Mk IV, a split-cane rod designed by Walker specifically for playing (and hopefully landing) very large carp.

Walker, who was a Cambridge-educated engineer, did more than anyone to bring a scientific mind to the pursuit of carp and other fish. Many anglers admire his innovations; others feel he perhaps overdid the scientific side of things and thereby diminished the mystery of angling which has always been a major part of its attraction.

Unjustly forgotten book

Days and Nights of Salmon Fishing in the Tweed (1843) by William Scrope. Featuring *A Short Account of the Natural History and Habits of the Salmon, Instructions to Sportsmen, Anecdotes*, etc., all manner of tips for fishing England's 'great salmon river' are described.

William Scrope was an English sportsman, artist, and writer. He published just two books: *The Art of Deerstalking* and *Days and Nights of Salmon Fishing in the Tweed.* They were illustrated with plates by the well-known artists Edwin Landseer, Charles Landseer, David Wilkie, and William Simson, among others.

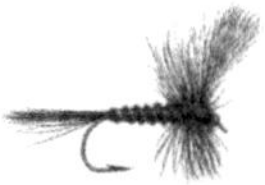

Famous angler

THE MAN credited with creating the strict rules around chalk stream dry fly fishing was Frederic Halford (1844–1914) a businessman who retired aged just forty-five to devote himself to fishing for the rest of his long life.

He started his fishing career as a boy on London's Serpentine Lake in Hyde Park and reputedly caught a 9lb brown trout from the Thames. But chalk stream fishing was his great love.

He began fly fishing experimenting with a fry fly on the River Wandle in South West London (back then still a rural area) and fished there from 1868–1881 by which time the relentless spread of London had reached and largely destroyed the river at least as a trout stream. Halford turned his attentions to the Test and the Itchen and he fished them when they were at their peak of perfection – before pollution from millions of cars, excessive abstraction by agri-farmers and encroaching urban development. Halford did much to establish the idea that gentlemen only fished the upstream dry fly.

Halford wrote many books but the two most famous are *Dry-Fly Fishing in Theory and Practice* (1889) and *Floating Flies and How to Dress Them* (1886).

✵

> The charm of fishing is that it is the pursuit of what is elusive but attainable, a perpetual series of occasions for hope.
>
> John Buchan 1875–1940 (author of *The Thirty-Nine Steps*)

Cold comfort

DESPITE BEING widely distributed across the world the Arctic char is one of Britain's rarest fish species. It lives only in a few very deep glacial lakes but has been re-stocked, for example, in Lake Padarn in Wales. No other fish species across the world lives so far north. It is the sole fish species found in Lake Hazern in the Arctic north of Canada.

✵

Ancholme eel and Witham pike,
In all England is none like.

Lincolnshire proverb

Many sided floats

THE STICK float is traditionally used for trotting small baits in fast-flowing water; the Avon, a straight stemmed float with a thicker cork body fitted towards the top, is used on deeper fast-flowing water using heavier baits than are used with the stick float. The waggler – a straight stemmed float with bulbous section towards the bottom – is attached to the line by the bottom only, unlike the stick and Avon, both of which are attached top and bottom. The bubble float – a plastic ball about the size of a large marble. Tied on the line above the bait the bubble jinks to left or right indicating a bite. Chubbers are short, thick floats designed for shallower, faster water using heavy baits.

Old version

Give a man a fish and you feed him for a day.
Teach a man to fish and you feed him for life.

New version

Give a man a fish and you feed him for a day.
Teach a man to fish and he'll cause an extinction.

Horse hair leaders and how to use them

HORSE HAIR was used for centuries to make what we now call leaders – the fine monofilament tied at the end of a fly line and to which the artificial (sometimes real) fly is attached. For coarse fishing a long level main line often made of thick silk was used with the horse hair tied to the end of it. The last few feet of fine horsehair line would then have a hook attached.

Horse hair was very carefully chosen to make those final few feet of all important line. White horses were usually chosen and the hairs were taken from the horse's tail to ensure the longest possible piece of hair and to reduce the number of knots needed to tie a decent hook length.

White horses were said to have slightly stronger hairs than piebalds or roans or black horses, and geldings were always chosen rather than mares or stallions. The process of gelding was believed to make the animal grow stronger hairs.

A single horse hair was perfectly adequate for gudgeon, dace or even roach fishing. Two or three hairs were plaited together for bigger fish such as chub and larger bream and carp. For barbel or salmon as many as a dozen hairs might be woven together. Mares were not used because they tended to urinate on their tails thus weakening the hairs!

Queen Elizabeth the Queen Mother

ACCORDING TO at least one royal historian, Queen Elizabeth the Queen Mother was a passionate salmon angler – but this is hardly a surprise as the Royal Family's private 50,000-acre estate at Balmoral includes 10 miles of one of the best salmon fishing rivers in the world – the River Dee.

Apparently, the Queen Mother slipped while wading on one occasion and had to be rescued by her gillie. As she was hauled out of the water she said, 'This is rather fun, isn't it?'

Feeding frenzy eyes

FRESHWATER FISH lack eyelids, which is why in general they dislike bright weather. Sharks are an exception – they have an eye covering called a nictitating membrane which comes into use to protect the shark's sight when it gets into a feeding frenzy with other sharks.

Rock climber

FISH EXPLOIT an extraordinary range of breeding behaviours. The rock-climbing goby, for example, has adapted fins to enable it to cling to wet, slippery rocks while it climbs as much as 30ft through powerful waterfalls to reach its spawning grounds. Only a small percentage of the fish reach the top – but enough make it to breed and then their young descend the waterfall and the cycle continues.

Opposites

SALMON AND sea trout are anadromous, meaning they return from the sea to freshwater to breed. The European eel does the opposite – it is catadromous meaning it leaves freshwater to spawn in the sea.

Valuable fish

THE COELACANTH had long been known from fossils. This large lobe-finned fish was assumed to have become extinct around 63 million years ago. Then in 1938 a specimen was discovered in a fish market in South Africa. Since then, around eighty coelacanths have been caught. The irony is that fishermen now target the coelacanths as they are valuable – every museum in the world wants one, which may push this very rare species to extinction. A coelacanth in good condition might cost £50,000. That figure is dwarfed by the £1 million-plus occasionally paid by the Japanese for a very large bluefin tuna.

Hobbs' choice

EDWARDS HOBBS, the author of *Trout of the Thames* published in 1947, claims to have landed an astonishing 878 trout from the Thames each weighing more than 3lb between the years 1890 and

1945. Hobbs also claims to have lost a 20lb-plus trout – it escaped right at the net after his gillie made a bad job of netting the fish.

Hobbs wrote that the biggest rod-caught Thames trout weighed a little over 14lb 9oz, but he mentions a 17-pounder netted from the lower Thames. Trout have always occurred naturally in the Thames but the big fish caught by Hobbs were probably stocked fish – in the 1880s, for example, tens of thousands of Scottish trout from Loch Leven were introduced to the river.

Rod and line Thames salmon

ONLY A handful of salmon have been caught on rod and line in the Thames in modern times. In 1992 student Michael Hargrave caught a 14½lb salmon at Maidenhead on a spinner and a fifty-year-old cane rod. In the same year, 114 salmon were recorded moving up through the fish pass at Molesey Weir. The problem with the Thames is that all the streams that run into the river are unsuitable for the salmon to spawn, so even those that make it up the river find that conditions are unsuitable for them to reproduce.

Illingworth spinning reel

THE SPINNING reel – a major improvement so far as casting any distance is concerned – began life in 1905 with inventor Alfred Illingworth. Instead of line being released only when a drum on which it is stored was turned (the basic principle of the multiplier and centrepin reels) the spinning reel or threadline reel, as it was once known, uses an arm to gather the line around a drum.

With the mechanical arm lifted out of the way, the reel would release line with minimum friction allowing light baits and lures to be cast a considerable distance. Purists dislike the spinning reel however as it creates more mechanical distance between angler and quarry when playing a fish. The sensitivity of the centrepin to a running fish is still today unmatched by any other reel.

Spitter

ARCHERFISH HAVE learned how to use spit to bring down their food in the form of insects on branches above the water. They can shoot accurately at insects up to 1m away and as they shoot from under the water they can even allow for refraction caused by the water. It's a difficult calculation involving an instinctive knowledge of physics!

There are ten species of archerfish spread across Southeast Asia where they inhabit freshwater rivers and streams but also brackish estuarine environments and mangrove swamps.

So how does the shooting mechanism work? Well, the archerfish has a groove in its mouth that fills with water; the fish then positions itself so its mouth is a fraction above the surface of the water. It then compresses its gills rapidly to force water through and out of the mouth groove. Incredibly, the water at the back of the groove moves through the air slightly faster than the water at the front of the column so that by the time the water reaches its prey the water at the back has caught up with the water at the front to create a blob powerful enough to engulf the insect and make it fall into the water. In tests, archerfish almost never miss!

✵

No human … was ever so free as a fish.

John Ruskin (1819–1900)

Lightbulb fish

ANGLERS IN search of giants of the sea such as marlin and sailfish look out for feeding fish by trying to spot a curious neon glow, which develops along their flanks when they are in the mood to feed. It is almost as if a lightbulb begins to glow inside these fish. It is in fact a form of bioluminescence, the chemicals generating light are akin to the light emitted by many sea creatures that live in the deepest parts of the oceans.

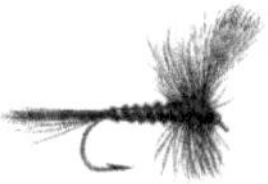

Catfish adaptations

CATFISH, NAMED for their whisker-like barbels, exhibit a range of special adaptations across a wide range of species: the gaff-topsail, for example, creates vibrations to communicate with other fish by rhythmically rubbing its fins against its swim bladder; the marine striped eel catfish is so venomous it can kill; the Amazon River toothpick catfish attacks humans foolish enough to swim where they live by swimming up their urethras. Perhaps strangest of all are the four species of Indian catfish in the genus *Holanis*. They grow to a maximum of 6cm, are blind and colourless and live entirely underground.

Thunderstorm trout

TROUT NEVER stir when the air is surcharged with electricity, such as it is just before a thunderstorm. It appears entirely to paralyse them.

P. B. M. Allan, *Trout Heresy*, 1936

Tidal trout

A CORRESPONDENT of *The Field* magazine of 6 October 1927 records catching in tidal waters, a brown trout of around a quarter of a pound in fine condition which, while being unhooked, disgorged a herring of about three and a half inches long.

Three on at the same time

A CORRESPONDENT to *Angling* magazine for July 1974 describes hooking a small perch which was taken by a much larger perch while it was being reeled in. The bigger perch was then taken by a massive pike. After a short tussle the angler knew he would lose, the big pike and the big perch removed themselves from the end of the line leaving the small perch which the angler reeled in and then released. It swam off apparently uninjured.

Quite a catch

FISHING AT the end of the nineteenth century on the Thames at Richmond, an angler records (in a letter to *The Field*) catching a pike, followed by a dace, a roach, a flounder, an eel, a bream, a chub and then a trout. All caught within the space of an hour and on small red worms.

Trout from the Kennet and Avon Canal

I HAVE, moreover, had proofs that the canal holds secrets, and is slow to divulge them. I fished it for two or three years before I had an inkling that there were any trout in it. The thought of trout had never even occurred to me. Why should they leave a noble habitation like the Kennet to take up inferior lodgings in an almost streamless piece of water full of pike?

Then one August day, when a breeze was ruffling the surface, I went out to spin for perch with a small Devon minnow, and was presently amazed to see a big trout follow the bait right across the canal almost to my feet. He did not take it, but his appearance opened new vistas, and a more careful watch was kept on the likely spots.

Eventually the fact was established that there were one or two trout scattered along the length of canal between the two locks, and that they ought to be fished for. Accordingly, I fished for them, and a tedious business it was, flogging away with Alexandras and the like on windy days, with never a rise to cheer one up, and with a constantly growing doubt whether the fish did not hasten to leave the canal whenever the locks were opened to give entrance or exit to a barge.

At last, I practically gave up the idea of catching one, and should have had no story to tell but for a lucky accident. One morning during what was supposed to be the mayfly season – Arctic weather was making it a thing of naught – I made my way in rain and wind along the canal to the river, in the fond hope of seeing a few mayflies and a rising trout. As I went, I suddenly saw a trout in the canal. It was in a deepish pool clear of weeds right out in the middle, but not very far from the sill of a small overflow weir, which serves to carry surplus water from the canal, when it is very full, under a light towing-bridge to the river on the other side of a meadow. When the canal is full it causes a very slight stream above this weir, and no doubt the fish was there to take advantage of it.

I could not get him to look at anything then, but after a blank day by the river and a consolatory cup of tea, I attached a gold-bodied grilse fly to the end of a mayfly cast, and came back to the canal. Several likely looking spots, still ruffled by a brisk but diminishing wind, were fished carefully over without sign of a fish, and at last, about 7 p.m., the haunt of the trout was reached. But the whole pool, some thirty yards in length, was covered without result, and it looked as though the fish was sulky or else had moved elsewhither.

But whither would he have been likely to go?

One part of a canal is much like another, and this was more favourable as an ending-ground than most. Only one spot had been left untried, and this was the yard or two of clear water above the sill of the little weir, not more than two feet deep, and overlooked by every passer-by as he crossed the bridge. Still, there was more stream in this spot than anywhere; no one had crossed the bridge for some time, and it was worth trying. Kneeling, I worked the fly across the spot. It had just reached the corner nearest to me when something seized it like a tiger, and dashed off wildly for the deeper water outside. A brisk fight followed, complicated by weeds, rough gusts of wind, and finally by an obstinate knuckle-joint on the landing-net; but at last, all went smoothly, and in due course I knelt upon the towpath gloating over a beautifully spotted, small-headed trout that looked as if it ought to weigh three and a half pounds.

H. T. Sheringham, *An Open Creel*, 1910

Trout's ancestral memory

THE PASSING of centuries has not removed the trout's ancestral memory. He came from the sea and he will return to the sea whenever and wherever he finds the descent to be of advantage to him. Where he inhabits land-locked waters, there Dame Nature has made him happy in his surroundings; where the chalk stream is his abode, there he remains, so long as the food supply is plentiful and never failing. But whenever he finds himself in a river where food is scarce, then, with the sureness of instinct, he will make his way downstream till he reaches those waters wherein food is in abundance.

He does not forget the river: it is a haven where he may breed unmolested, and in the shelter of its banks he may recover from the exertions of spawning, secure from the larger enemies that are for ever hunting him in the open sea.

Mr F. G. Richmond, writing in *The Salmon and Trout* magazine records that a rapid Welsh river was stocked with large yearling rainbows; they were caught the following year running about 1lb apiece; the year afterwards they vanished and were caught by trout netsmen in the estuary below, running from 2lb to 3lb. In this case the inference appears obvious that food became short and that the fish naturally went downstream in search of better pasturage.

Eric Parker et al., *Fine Angling for Coarse Fish*, 1930

Tame cormorant

THE SAME gentleman caught in the Thames a Pike weighing 9lb with a moorhen in its gullet, by which it was being suffocated; and on another occasion a fish of 5lb that had one of 3lb half-swallowed, but made, notwithstanding, an effort to take his spinning-bait, and was hooked foul in the attempt.

Since the above was put into type, I have been favoured by Captain S. H. Salvin with a curious pendant to one of these anecdotes. Captain Salvin had until recently in his possession a tame Cormorant, which had been for many years trained to catch fish for his master by diving – amongst other odd captures made by it being that of a Water-hen, which it secured and brought to the bank after an exciting chase. Within the last few months, however, the career of the feathered angler has been tragically cut short: while diving one day as usual, he was seized by a jack pike, which was itself choked in its endeavours to swallow him. The weight of this Jack was only 7lb.

Thomas Stoddart, *Angler's Companion*, 1892

Chapter 6

ECCENTRIC

Naked in the nets

IN CAMBODIA, if a netsman be unsuccessful, he strips naked and withdraws a short distance: then strolling up to the net, as if he saw it not, he lets himself be caught in the meshes, whereupon he calls out, 'What is this? I fear I am caught.' Such procedure is believed to attract the fish efficaciously and to ensure a good haul.

William Radcliffe, *Fishing from the Earliest Times*, 1921

Bees for chub

THE BEST bait in June, July, and August, for Chub, is the humble-bee, during the day, and late in the evening, a large white moth, bred in willow trees; it is called the Owl-Fly, from its resembling an owl in the face and head. Artificial moths, bees, butterflies, cockchafers, grasshoppers, &c. may be purchased at the tackle-shops.

I have had much success (particularly in the river Lea) in whipping with a humble-bee, both with the natural and artificial; this is my usual bait, till towards dusk, for Chub, then I use a small black fly, which will also catch Dace.

Thomas Salter, *The Art of Angling*, 1833

✻

Fishing: A frank resumption of palaeolithic life without the spur of palaeolithic hunger.

Graham Wallace, *Human Nature in Politics*, 1908

Fraudulent perch

SOME VERY large so-called perch have proved to be bass or sea-perch, fish which will ascend the brackish waters of tidal rivers; a monster '10¾lb perch' from one of the Norfolk Broads, shown at the 1883 International Fisheries Exhibition turned out to be a sea bass, with five dark stripes painted on the body.

Alfred Jardine, *Pike and Perch*, 1897

Fishing in a sewer

IN THE early 1970s the teenage anglers' grapevine in north London was abuzz with stories about big fish caught in a sewage outlet in Tottenham. Near-record roach, dace and gudgeon were being caught in large numbers where the outlet flowed quickly into the river Lea. One dace was so big it would have undoubtedly broken the British record – the lucky captor felt it would not be appropriate to try to claim the record, however, because fishing a sewage outlet was almost certainly unlawful! The water had been treated but there was clearly something in it that made the fish grow fast!

Angling magazine, Letters, June 1979

Cesspit roach

OTHER ODD spots for fishing have been reported – one young man on a Surrey farm took a few roach from a farm pond and put

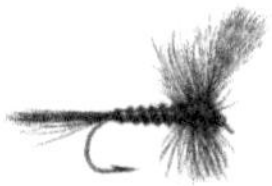

them in a disused cesspit where they grew and multiplied, so much so that the cesspit offered better fishing than the farm pond!

The Angler's Notebook and Naturalist's Record, 1880

Beating about the bush

WHEN YOU come first to the river in the morning, with your rod beat upon the bushes or boughs which hang over the water, and by their falling upon the water you will see what sorts of flies are there in greatest numbers; if divers sorts, and equal in number, try them all, and you will quickly find which they most desire.

Robert Venables *The Experienced Angler*, 1662

✵

Bleak probably take their name from the weather experienced by the Thames trout fisher!

H. T. Sheringham, *Fishing: Its Cause Treatment and Cure*, 1925

The Angler's Lament

At a brandling once gudgeons would gape,
But they seem to have alter'd their forms, now:
Have they taken advice of the Council of Nice,
And rejected the Diet of Worms, now?

Anon

Sound as a roach

IN HAZLITT'S *Collection of Proverbial Phrases*, we find the entries 'as sound as a roach' and 'as sound as a trout'. It would seem that our ancestors considered fish, in general, as a type of all that is healthy, the roach and trout being specially singled out for this distinction.

It becomes a question how old this idea may be.

Without giving any explicit answer to this, I can shew that fish were proverbially 'whole' as early as the fifteenth century. I have met with two curious examples of this, and I dare say more may be found.

In the *Romance of Alexander*, as edited by Stevenson for the Roxburgh Club, we have the story of Alexander taking a chill by bathing in a river, and how he was healed by a drink administered by his physician Philip.

Alexander was warned that Philip designed to poison him, but he drank the potion without hesitation. 'As fast was he fysch-hale,' i.e. he was at once as whole as a fish.

In the *Chevalere Assigne*, edited by H. H. Gibbs, we have a still more startling story of a goldsmith, who had five gold chains, and who actually warranted them by declaring that they were all 'fysh-hole'. This singular use of the proverb shews how widely and loosely it was applied.

The Angler's Notebook and Naturalist's Record, 1880

Violinist hit by fish

IT'S NOW quite common in London to see geese flying overhead or swans; even, occasionally, a rarity such as a cormorant. Along the Thames, right into the heart of the City, herons now stalk the shallows and various wildlife bodies tell us that owls roost in Parliament Square while kestrels hover above the Commercial Road.

In the nineteenth century things were very different, as pollution caused by millions of coal fires – not to mention heavy industry – meant there was far less wildlife than today.

But having said that, London's bigger parks have always provided a haven for wildlife, which is why reports of duck wandering across Kensington High Street with their ducklings coming along behind were quite common.

Far less common was the bizarre wildlife encounter in Kensington reported in a Victorian newspaper. A young violinist was walking home one autumn evening after what the delightfully old-fashioned newspaper reporter described as 'a musical engagement involving the celebrated Mr Bach'. She was halfway up Kensington Church Street when she was struck by what she later described to the newspaper reporter as 'a terrific blow to the side of the head'.

One of the witnesses who helped the injured woman into a local house where brandy was administered (much, apparently, to the delight of the young violinist) described an extraordinary circumstance that almost certainly accounted for the blow.

When the witness had run up to the prostrate violinist he spotted a moderately sized fish lying on the pavement nearby. Being a fisherman, he knew that this was not the sort of fish one buys at a fishmonger. It was in fact a roach, a common British freshwater fish, but completely inedible.

The witness told the newspaper that at first, he could not understand how the fish came to be lying in the street, but in helping the injured woman to her feet he noticed something very odd indeed. The woman's head and the shoulder of her coat were dusted here and there with fish scales. The scales were without question from the dead roach found at the scene.

When the newspaper reporter compiled his report on the incident, he quoted a professor of zoology who stated that Miss Wadham was almost certainly felled by a roach dropped by a passing bird, possibly a heron or cormorant.

Net the visitors

A FORMER editor of *Angling* magazine worked in the first-floor office with a small balcony overlooking the street below. When visitors pressed the office doorbell outside, he would jump on to his balcony and drop a long keepnet over the unsuspecting visitor's head.

Shark harpoons

ANGLING AUTHOR Trevor Housby regularly attempted to harpoon sharks from his small fishing boat off the south coast of England.

Assailed by arrows

THE ZOOLOGIST Peter Simon Pallas (1741–1811) speaks of a carp taken in the Volga which measured five feet; Valmont de Bomare, of another served at the table of Prince Conti, at Offenburg, weighing forty-five pounds; and another monster was dragged from the Oder, near Frankfurt, in 1711, of the incredible size of nine feet long by three deep, the weight of which was seventy pounds. Jovius speaks of carp in the Larian Lake (Como) of two hundred pounds, which were assailed by arrows shot from a crossbow or by harpoons with a string attached; adding, that in using these weapons it was necessary to strike the fish against the scales, otherwise they would glance off without penetrating the flesh.

The tenacity of life exhibited by carp is another remarkable circumstance in their physiology: not only will they flourish for a very long term of years under favourable conditions for growth and development, but they have been not unfrequently found alive in the muddy bottom of an almost empty pond, where their bodies, potted and preserved, assume sometimes very strange forms, being gradually moulded into the shape of the hole in which they lay.

Charles Badham, *Fish Tattle*, 1854

Naughty trick

There was a little fellow once,
And Harry was his name,
And many a naughty trick he had,
I tell it to his shame.
He minded not his friends' advice
But followed his own wishes,
And one most cruel trick of his
Was that of catching fishes.
And many a little fish he caught,
And pleased was he to look,
To see him writhe in agony
And struggle on a hook.
At last, when having caught enough,

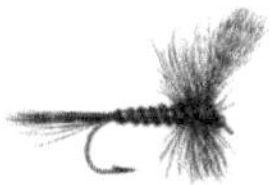

And also tired himself,
He hastened home, intending there
To put them on a shelf.

Percival Leigh, *Jack the Giant Killer*, 1850

Confessions of a duffer

THERE IS no false modesty in the confidence with which I esteem myself a duffer, at fishing. Some men are born duffers; others, unlike persons of genius, become so by an infinite capacity for not taking pains. Others, again, among whom I would rank myself, combine both these elements of incompetence. Nature, that made me enthusiastically fond of fishing, gave me thumbs for fingers, short-sighted eyes, indolence, carelessness, and a temper which (usually sweet and angelic) is goaded to madness by the laws of matter and of gravitation.

For example: when another man is caught up in a branch he disengages his fly; I jerk at it till something breaks. As for carelessness, in boyhood I fished, by preference, with doubtful gut and knots ill-tied; it made the risk greater, and increased the excitement if one did hook a trout. I can't keep a fly-book. I stuff the flies into my pockets at random, or stick them into the leaves of a novel, or bestow them in the lining of my hat or the case of my rods. Never, till 1890, in all my days did I possess a landing-net.

If I can drag a fish up a bank, or over the gravel, well; if not, he goes on his way rejoicing. On the Test I thought it seemly to carry a landing-net. It had a hinge, and doubled up. I put the handle through a button-hole of my coat: I saw a big fish rising, I put a dry fly over him; the idiot took it. Upstream he ran, then downstream, then he yielded to the rod and came near me. I tried to unship my landing-net from my button-hole. Vain labour! I twisted and turned the handle, it would not budge. Finally, I stooped, and attempted to ladle the trout out with the short net; but he broke the gut, and went off.

A landing-net is a tedious thing to carry, so is a creel, and a creel is, to me, a superfluity. There is never anything to put in it. If I do catch a trout, I lay him under a big stone, cover him with leaves, and never find him again. I often break my top joint; so, as I never carry string,

I splice it with a bit of the line, which I bite off, for I really cannot be troubled with scissors and I always lose my knife. When a phantom minnow sticks in my clothes, I snap the gut off, and put on another, so that when I reach home I look as if a shoal of fierce minnows had attacked me and hung on like leeches.

When a boy, I was – once or twice – a bait-fisher, but I never carried worms in box or bag. I found them under big stones, or in the fields, wherever I had the luck. I never tie nor otherwise fasten the joints of my rod; they often slip out of the sockets and splash into the water. Mr Hardy, however, has invented a joint-fastening which never slips. On the other hand, by letting the joint rust, you may find it difficult to take down your rod.

When I see a trout rising, I always cast so as to get hung up, and I frighten him as I disengage my hook. I invariably fall in and get half-drowned when I wade, there being an insufficiency of nails in the soles of my brogues. My waders let in water, too, and when I go out to fish I usually leave either my reel, or my flies, or my rod, at home.

Perhaps no other man's average of lost flies in proportion to taken trout was ever so great as mine. I lose plenty, by striking furiously, after a series of short rises, and breaking the gut, with which the fish swims away. As to dressing a fly, one would sooner think of dressing a dinner. The result of the fly-dressing would resemble a small blacking-brush, perhaps, but nothing entomological.

Then why, a persevering reader may ask, do I fish?

Well, it is stronger than myself, the love of fishing; perhaps it is an inherited instinct, without the inherited power. I may have had a fishing ancestor who bequeathed to me the passion without the art. My vocation is fixed, and I have fished to little purpose all my days. Not for salmon, an almost fabulous and yet a stupid fish, which must be moved with a rod like a weaver's beam. The trout is more delicate and dainty – not the sea-trout, which any man, woman, or child can capture, but the yellow trout in clear water.

A few rises are almost all I ask for: to catch more than half a dozen fish does not fall to my lot twice a year. Of course, in a Sutherland loch one man is as good as another, the expert no better than the duffer. The fish will take, or they won't. If they won't, nobody can catch them; if they will, nobody can miss them. It is as simple as trolling a minnow from a boat in Loch Leven, probably the lowest possible form of angling. My ambition is as great as my skill is feeble; to capture big trout with the dry fly in the Test, that would content me, and nothing under that. But I can't see the natural fly on the water; I cannot see my own fly.

Let it sink or let it swim.

I often don't see the trout rise to me, if he is such a fool as to rise; and I can't strike in time when I do see him. Besides, I am unteachable to tie any of the orthodox knots in the gut; it takes me half an hour to get the gut through one of these newfangled iron eyes, and, when it is through, I knot it any way. The 'jam' knot is a name to me, and no more. That, perhaps, is why the hooks crack off so merrily. Then, if I do spot a rising trout, and if he does not spot me as I crawl like the serpent towards him, my fly always fixes in a nettle, a haycock, a rose-bush, or whatnot, behind me. I undo it, or break it, and put up another, make a cast, and, 'plop', all the line falls in with a splash that would frighten a crocodile. The fish's big black fin goes cutting the stream above ...

Angling Sketches, Andrew Lang, 1895

Gut, hair, and silk

HOW TO make Gut and Horse-Hair Lines, single and twisted; their different qualities considered. How to place shot on the same, and fix them to the Rod, try the strength of Hooks, &c.

Fishing-lines are made of gut, twisted horse or cow's hair, and single horse hair; also of silk and mohair, or of silk alone, either twisted or platted; those made of gut are the strongest, the twisted hair cheapest, and the single horse-hair the finest. You may make a fine line, by having half single hair at bottom, the other part two hairs twisted. The gut, or silkworm gut, is made or manufactured from the intestines, or gut of the silkworm, and is the strongest substance for its circumference, known by the Angler, and makes a line superior to anything else, the natural colour of which is better than much that is stained.

The young angler will find a line of about four yards in length the most useful, either to fish with or without a winch, as he must note that the line is unmanageable if longer than the rod. In shotting the line to sink the float, place them close together, within three inches of the bottom loop of the line; to which loop fix the loop of the hair or gut that the hook is tied to, and always put one or two shot on them above the middle, which will keep your bait down, and cause the whole to swim steady. However, when you make a line, either of silk, gut, or hair, it always must be finest at bottom, where the hook is fastened, and very gradually increasing in bulk or thickness to the top. When you place shot on the line, do it with a pair of pliers, which is the best and easiest method; some fasten them with their teeth, but it is a bad practice, for they often bite the hair or gut through, which causes much delay and vexation, particularly if it happens while you are fishing.

Thomas Salter, *The Art of Angling*, 1833

A most eccentric angler

FRANK BUCKLAND (1820–1880) was one of the most eccentric anglers who ever lived. He was also the son of the Dean of Westminster, William Buckland (known as the Dinosaur Dean).

Frank collected stuffed and live animals, including fish. When one of his live animals died – it might be a hippopotamus or a mouse – he usually ate it. He developed some extremely effective ways to preserve dead animals, but he did it using highly poisonous chemicals that seriously damaged his health. When he wasn't stuffing animals, Buckland spent his time fishing for trout and salmon. Fishing was a pursuit he'd started while at Winchester School. It had often got him into serious trouble because whenever he felt like it, he would set off for the riverbank without telling anyone. When he returned, he was invariably thrashed but it never dampened his enthusiasm. He was also often found asleep with a dead trout or a barbel lying next to him. He was interested at an early age in the process of putrefaction and kept dead fish and other animals until they rotted away.

In middle age Buckland's knowledge of fish – live and dead – had developed to such an extent that he was appointed Her Majesty's Inspector of Fisheries. On one never-to-be-forgotten day he put up a sign by a weir that was still waiting for a salmon ladder to be built into it. The sign, designed for the benefit of any fish stuck below the weir, read: 'No road at present over the weir. Go downstream, take the first turning to the right and you will find good travelling water upstream and no jumping required.'

Buckland was a fanatical fisherman and after checking the weir and putting up his sign he set off to fish. Baffled by his lack of success he stripped off – it was a very cold day in February – and lowered himself into the fastest part of the river to see what it felt like to be a salmon and to see if he could at least begin the swim against the current and towards the salmon ladder.

When he climbed out, he was heard to mumble: 'Good God! How on earth do they do it?'

This dip into the freezing water combined with his reckless use of numerous noxious substances led Buckland to an early grave. He died aged just fifty-four. On his deathbed fish were still on his mind and his last words were: 'God is so good, so very good, to the little fishes that I do not believe he would let their inspector suffer shipwreck.'

Cultivate your luck

ON THE subject of carp … I take my stand entirely on luck. To the novice I would say, 'Cultivate your luck. Prop it up with omens and signs of good purport. Watch for magpies on your path. Form the habit of avoiding old women who squint. Throw salt over your left shoulder. Touch wood … be on friendly terms with a black cat … turn your money under a new moon … don't start on a Friday.

H. T. Sheringham, *Coarse Fishing*, 1912

*

The carp … a salmon with brains.

Faddist, *Memorable Coarse Fish*, 1953

How to make horse hair lines

TO TEACH the way or manner how to make a line, were time lost, it being so easy and ordinary; yet to make the line well, handsome, and to twist the hair even and neat, makes the line strong. For if one hair be long and another short, the short one receiveth no strength from the long one, and so breaketh, and then the other, as too weak, breaks also; therefore you must twist them slowly, and in the twisting, keep them from entangling together, which hinders their right plaiting or bedding. Further, I do not like the mixing of silk or thread with hair, but if you please, you may, to make the line strong, make it all of silk, or thread, or hair, as strong as you please, and the lowest part of the smallest lute or viol strings, which I have proved to be very strong, but will quickly rot in the water, you may however help that in having new and strong ones to change for those that decay; but as to hair, the most usual matter whereof lines are made, I like sorrel, white, and grey best; sorrel in muddy and boggy rivers, and both the latter for clear waters. I never could find such virtue or worth in other colours, to give them so high praise as some do, yet if any other have worth in it, I must yield it to the pale or watery green, and if you fancy that, you may dye it thus. Take a pottle of allum water, and a large handful of marigolds, boil them until a yellow scum arise, then take half a pound of green copperas, and as much verdegrease, beat them into a fine powder, then put those with the hair into the allum water, set all to cool for twelve hours, then take out the hair and lay it to dry.

Robert Venables, *The Experienced Angler*, 1662

The first fish which I bring up
In the name of Christ,
King of the Elements,
The poor man shall have for his need:
And the King of the Fishers,
The brave Peter,
He will after it give me his blessing.
Columba, tender in every distress,
And Mary fair, the endowed of grace,
Encompass ye us to the fishing bank of ocean,
And still ye to us the crest of the waves!

Ancient Irish prayer

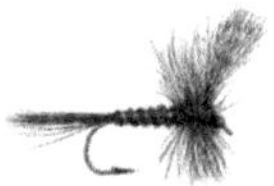

Biggest ever

THE BIGGEST carp ever caught anywhere on rod and line, as of 2025, was a mirror carp weighing just over 112½lb. It was caught in a Hungarian lake in November 2018, by Michel Schoenmakers.

Trap door to the lake

PLATFORMS SUPPLIED by tall piles stand in the middle of the lake, which are approached from the land by a narrow single stage. At first the piles were fixed by all citizens, but since that time the custom that has prevailed about fixing them is this, every man drives in three for each wife he marries. Now the men all have many wives apiece, and this is the way they live. Each has his own hut (wherein he dwells) on one of the platforms, and each has a trap door, giving access to the lake beneath: their wont is to tie the baby children by the foot with a string, to save them from rolling into the water. They feed their horses and other beasts on fish, which abound in the lake in such a degree that a man has only to open his trap door, and let down a basket by a rope into the water, and then wait a very short time, when he draws it up quite full of fish.

Herodotus, *Histories, c.* 430 BC

Physician fish

THE TENCH has a few teeth in his jaws, and is of the Carp species, but not a very handsome Fish in shape, being short and thick, and when of a large size nearly as broad as they are long; their fins and tail are large, and of a purple violet colour; their scales are very small and close, and of a greenish gold colour, and the whole body is covered with a balsamic quality, healing the wounded and sick of all the finny race; for which purpose, writers say, the sick and wounded rub themselves against the Tench, and receive a cure: this is the general and received opinion, and, in consequence, the Tench is honoured with the name of the Physician, and it is said they are respected, even by the all-devouring Pike.

Whether the forbearance of the Pike arises from respect to the healing qualities of the Tench, or is to be attributed to a dislike of the slimy matter on its body, I know not, but I believe the Tench is perfectly free from the persecution of Jack and Pike; for I have never taken one that has been at all mutilated in its fins, tail, or any other part; or with any of those wounds or scars on the body, which are so frequently met with by the Angler, among the small Fish he takes. The Eel also foregoes his voracity, in regard to the Tench, both by night and day.

Thomas Salter, *The Art of Angling*, 1833

Mouth-breeders

THERE ARE more than 1,760 different species of freshwater cichlid. The cichlids are ray-finned fish found across India, Africa and the Middle East.

Every year new species are discovered and scientists reckon there are probably at least 2,000 species, so many are yet to be discovered. Cichlids are hugely successful although many species are at risk of extinction.

Their success may be partly down to their habit of guarding their eggs rather than as with so many fish species simply laying enough eggs to ensure that, once abandoned, enough eggs survive to continue the species. Many cichlids are also mouth-brooders – they protect their eggs and young by keeping them in their mouths when danger threatens.

Fish with crazy names

THE BOGUE, a sea fish occasionally caught in UK waters has the curious Latin name *Boops boops*.

Other odd-named fish include:

- Bombay duck (*Harpadon nehereus*)
- Bony-eared assfish (*Acanthonus armatus*)
- Boxing crab (*Lybia tessellata*)

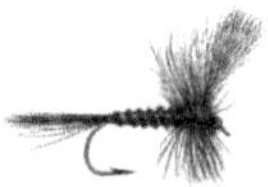

- Coffinfish (*Chaunax endeavouri*)
- Daggernose shark (*Isogomphodon oxyrhynchus*)
- Dumb gulper shark (*Centrophorus harrissoni*)
- Earmuff wrasse (*Halichoeres melasmapomus*)
- Jack Dempsey fish (*Rocio octofasciata*)
- Lipstick dottyback (*Photocorynus spiniceps*)
- Lumpsucker fish (*Cyclopterus lumpus*)
- Nervous shark (*Carcharhinus cautus*)
- Obese dragonfish (*Opostomias micripnus*)
- Psychedelic frogfish (*Histiophryne psychedelica*)
- Red-lipped batfish (*Ogcocephalus darwini*)
- Sarcastic fringehead (*Neoclinus blanchardi*)
- Slippery dick wrasse (*Halichoeres bivittatus*)
- Slobbering catfish (*Brachyplatystoma platynemum*)

Dogfish swords

CEREMONIAL NAVY swords in the UK have dogfish skin wrapped around the part that the swordsman grips – this has been done for centuries. The rough texture of the dogfish skin means that in the heat of battle with his hands sweating profusely, the swordsman can still keep a firm grip.

Classifying fish

THE SYSTEM of classifying fish species (and all other species on Earth) was largely invented by the Swedish naturalist Carl Linnaeus (1707–78). The first edition of his *Systema Naturae* was printed in the Netherlands in 1735. The book used for the first time binomials – an animal is given a generic name and specific name. We still use this system today – hence our common fish such as the gudgeon (*Gobio gobio*) or pike (*Esox lucius*) all have binomials.

The German poet Goethe wrote of Linnaeus: 'With the exception of William Shakespeare and Baruch Spinoza, I know no one among the no longer living who has influenced me more strongly.'

Curiously the type specimen for *Homo sapiens* – ourselves – is Linnaeus himself!

Best-selling fishing book of all

ARTIST BERNARD Venables (1907–2001) wrote and illustrated the best-selling fishing book of all time. *Mr Crabtree Goes Fishing* sold around 4 million copies as of 2024. The book was written and drawn while Venables was employed at the *Daily Mirror* – the paper claimed ownership of the copyright and Venables received none of the considerable royalties.

Purist dry fly

FISHING TECHNIQUES vary enormously. The ultimate purist must be the dry fly fisher. He only ever casts upstream (downstream is considered cheating) always imitates a real fly and must not let his fly sink. Experts wander the banks of English chalk streams waiting to see a fish rising. They work out what it is eating – the natural fly – and then tie an imitation of that exact fly to their line and cast it just above the rising fish. If everything works – the line doesn't fall heavily, or get caught in a bush – the fish will unsuspectingly take the fly and the purist hooks his trout.

Returns

MORE THAN 80 per cent of all fish in the UK are now returned unharmed to the water after being caught by an angler.

Thick lines work for tench

JUST PRIOR to World War One, I was staying at a house whose park bordered a stretch of the Kennet and Avon canal where there were numbers of Tench. These only seemed to bite for about a month,

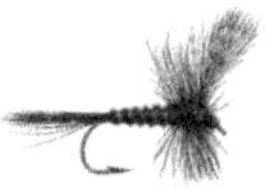

but when they did every rod in the house was hauled out and everyone turned out to fish for Tench on fine evenings.

When bubbles started rising from the bottom in numerous places it was a signal that the fish were looking for food. We all used float tackle baited with a large lobworm, and the float was adjusted so that the bait just rested on the bottom. But the rest of our gear varied a good deal and ranged from very thick gut, used by a salmon angler because 'Tench run large', to the fine-drawn of the dry-fly man, because he held that Tench was, 'Shy fish, my boy.'

Besides this house party, one of the gardeners used always to appear as soon as the horticultural 'Dismiss' had sounded. Now this man invariably made up for lost time by beginning to catch fish almost at once and continuing this until, before long, he had more Tench than all the rest of us put together. The only difference between his tackle and ours was that instead of using some gut next the hook he merely fastened the latter, which was an eyed eel hook, directly to his reel line.

After he had for three consecutive evenings far surpassed our united scores, and seeing that the absence of gut was the only difference either in his way of fishing or his gear, I decided to copy him. My gut was removed and the reel line fastened directly to an eyed salmon hook (with a clove hitch because the line was too big for the eye), and this was baited and tossed out into the canal. After that I was catching fish for fish with Jim the gardener, whilst the finer tackle party were only getting a very occasional bite.

Probably the explanation of the discrepancy was that as the lines of both Jim and myself were rather dark tinted, they matched the canal bottom and were thus invisible to the Tench who came grubbing along looking for or scenting food. Gradually the rest of the party, even the dry-fly man, followed our example and then everyone had a pile of Tench … There was, however, one exception to this universal prosperity. A scientific roach fisher sometimes appeared and was absolute in his refusal to change from the white silk line which he always used for roach – 'If it's good for they roach it be good for thicker coddling Tenches,' was his ultimatum. He caught none.

H. Atwood Clark, *For Fishermen Only*, 1934

✵

Angling on a summer night,
When the moon-ray met the fairy
Tripping down a bank of light
To the sweet loch of St Mary;
Music floated sad and holy,
Every wild flower lent its tune,
And the sullen trout swam slowly
Like the shadow of a stone.

T. T. Stoddart

Wading stockings

WADING STOCKINGS after fishing should be turned inside out and hung up to dry in a back kitchen, or someplace which is warm without being hot. When the inside is dry, they can be reversed and dried on the outside. After being put away for some time they sometimes get hard and uncomfortable. They can be softened by being hung for an hour or two in the vicinity of the kitchen fire, close enough for them to get warm slowly, but not so close that they get hot. Brogues which have got hard and stiff, and painful to the feet, should be soaked in water before being put on. The socks, which are worn over the wading stockings to protect them from rubbing, should be looked to now and again, as they develop holes in the heels on slight provocation, after which they protect the wader no longer.

The Angler's Notebook and Naturalist's Record, 1880

French success

WE HAVE seen a Frenchman, even on the Thames (the home of barbel fishing), with nothing but a bit of twine for a line, and half of an old whalebone umbrella-rib for a rod, beat the best local anglers. The ground bait, wherewith he attracted the fish to his swim, however, was of a nature seldom employed by English anglers, and, consisted chiefly of stable refuse.

Francis Francis, *Reminiscences*, 1887

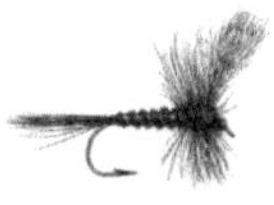

Chapter 7

WATER-LOGGED

Where to Fish, which provides information on fishing locations in the UK and Ireland, was first published in 1858. The ninety-second edition was released in 2011.

✵

To read about fishing is the next best thing to the road to the river.

Maurice Headlam, *Rod, Horn and Gun*, 1942

A big fish always has a hide

IN CASE of a very large fish, say of ten pounds and upwards, if I am using very fine tackle, I always like to let the punt loose, and, getting below the fish, take him into strange water, if possible, where he has no holt or hide to go to, and where he does not know the country.

For lack of this I have lost many a noble fish, as a big fish always has a hide, and sooner or later remembers and runs for it, when you may wish him 'good day'.

Francis Francis, *A Book on Angling*, 1867

Asthmatic eels

EVERYONE KNOWS, who may have tried the experiment, that to hold an eel with the naked hand is as abortive an attempt as detaining a pig by the tail, after it has been well soaped; or, in morals, to hold a knave to his word; hence the saying: 'He's an eel, and is off', but both rogue and eel may be held tight if we set about it the right way; hence the elliptic proverbial expression, 'Hold an eel with a fig-leaf.'

Aldrovandi states that horse-doctors gave small eels to their patients, in asthma; and as a purge, sometimes with advantage, a hint not thrown away, it seems, upon certain horse-jockeys, who, to improve the metal of the steeds they had to dispose of, adopted the same expedient.

The Angler's Notebook and Naturalist's Record, 1880

Crooks!

Crooks is English every inch,
From fishing he will never flinch,
He'll flourish his stick and turn a winch,
To fight or fish in the morning.

John Baddeley, *The London Angler's Book or Waltonian Chronicle*, 1834

The River Tivy

When as the salmon seeks a fresher stream to find
(Which yearly by the sea comes hither of his mind,
As he in reason grows), and stems the watery tract,
Where Tivy falling down doth make a cataract,
Forced by the rising rocks that there her course oppose,
As though within their bounds they meant her to enclose
Here, when the labouring fish doth at the foot arrive,
And knows that by his strength but vainly he doth strive
His tail takes in his teeth; and bending like a bow

That's to the compass drawn, aloft himself doth throw,
Then springing with his tail, as doth a little wand
That, bended end to end, and flirted from the hand,
Far off itself doth cast, so doth the salmon vault;
And if at first he fail, his second somersaut
He instantly assays; and from his nimble ring
Still yesting, never leaves until himself he fling
Above the streamful top of the surrounded heap.

Michael Drayton (1563–1631)

Almost unfishable loch

THE LOCH, to be plain, is almost unfishable. It is nearly round, and everywhere, except in a small segment on the eastern side, is begirt with reeds of great height. These reeds, again, grow in a peculiarly uncomfortable, quaggy bottom, which rises and falls, or rather which jumps and sinks when you step on it, like the seat of a very luxurious armchair. Moreover, the bottom is pierced with many springs, wherein if you set foot you shall have thrown your last cast.

By watching the loch when it is frozen, a man might come to learn something of the springs; but, even so, it is hard to keep clear of them in summer. Now the wind almost always blows from the west, dead against the little piece of gravelly shore at the eastern side, so that casting against it is hard work and unprofitable. On this day, by a rare chance, the wind blew from the east, though the sky at first was a brilliant blue, and the sun hot and fierce. I walked round to the east side, waded in, and caught two or three small fellows.

It was slow work, when suddenly there began the greatest rise of trout I ever saw in my life. From the edge of the loch as far as one could clearly see across it there was that endless plashing murmur, of all sounds in this world the sweetest to the ear.

Within the view of the eye, on each cast, there were a dozen trout rising all about, never leaping, but seriously and solemnly feeding. Now is my chance at last, I fancied; but it was not so – far from it. I might throw over the very noses of the beasts, but they seldom even glanced at the (artificial) fly. I tried them with Greenwell's Glory, with a March brown, with 'the woodcock wing and hare-lug', but it was almost to no purpose.

If one did raise a fish, he meant not business – all but 'a casual brute', which broke the already weakened part of a small 'glued-up' cane rod. I had to twist a piece of paper round the broken end, wet it, and push it into the joint, where it hung on somehow, but was not pleasant to cast with. From twelve to half-past one the gorging went merrily forward, and I saw what the fish were rising at.

The whole surface of the loch, at least on the east side, was absolutely peppered with large, hideous insects. They had big grey-white wings, bodies black as night, and brilliant crimson legs, or feelers, or whatever naturalists call them. The trout seemed as if they could not have too much of these abominable wretches, and the flies were blown across the loch, not singly, but in populous groups.

I had never seen anything like them in any hook-book, nor could I deceive the trout by the primitive dodge of tying a red thread round the shank of a dark fly. So I waded out, and fell to munching a frugal sandwich and watching Nature, not without a cigarette.

Now Nature is all very well. I have nothing to say against her of a Sunday, or when trout are not rising. But she was no comfort to me now. Smiling she gazed on my discomfiture.

The lovely lines of the hills, curving about the loch, and with their deepest dip just opposite where I sat, were all of a golden autumn brown, except in the violet distance. The grass of Parnassus grew thick and white around me, with its moonlight tint of green in the veins. On a hillside by a brook the countryfolk were winning their hay, and their voices reached me softly from far off. On the loch the marsh-fowl flashed and dipped, the wild ducks played and dived and rose; first circling high and higher, then, marshalled in the shape of a V, they made for Alemoor.

A solitary heron came quite near me, and tried his chance with the fish, but I think he had no luck. All this is pleasant to remember, and I made rude sketches in the fly-leaves of a copy of Hogg's poems, where I kept my flies. But what joy was there in this while the 'take' grew fainter and ceased at least near the shore? Out in the middle, where few flies managed to float, the trout were at it till dark.

But near shore there was just one trout who never stopped gorging all day. He lived exactly opposite the nick in the distant hills, and exactly a yard farther out than I could throw a fly. He was a big one, and I am inclined to think that he was the Devil. For, if I had stepped in deeper, and the water had come over my wading boots, the odds are that my frail days on earth would have been ended by a chill, and I knew this, and yet that fish went on tempting me to my ruin. I suppose I tried to reach him a dozen times, and cast a hundred, but it was to no avail.

At length, as the afternoon grew grey and chill, I pitched a rock at him, by way of showing that I saw through his fiendish guile, and I walked away.

Andrew Lang, *Angling Sketches*, 1891

Pike prices

DURING THE reign of Edward the First (i.e. towards the close of the thirteenth century) jack was so dear that few could afford to eat it; the price, says Mr Yarrell, was double that of salmon, and ten times higher than either turbot or cod. In 1466, pike was one of the chief dishes in the high church festival given by George Neville, Archbishop of York.

In Henry the Eighth's time these watery tyrants fetched as much again as house-lamb in February, and a very small pickerel would sell higher than a fat capon? In spite of the general wholesomeness of the fish, its roe has been said by some authorities to be deleterious, inducing (like that of the barbel) hypercatharsis and vomiting.

The Angler's Notebook and Naturalist's Record, 1880

✵

An old tradition in British fishing villages was to throw the first fish caught back into the sea as a sign of respect. A similar tradition saw fishermen return the biggest fish of the day in case it happened to be the King of the Fishes. Killing the King of the Fishes would bring endless bad luck.

✵

An American angler staying at the Ritz, at the turn of the nineteenth century, bet a friend that he could cast from his room overlooking the

Embankment into the River Thames. He succeeded and won the bet, allegedly.

Cardinal Wolsey's carp

A 37lb carp was found dead in Cardinal Wolsey's pond at Hampton Court when the water was drained during the 1914–18 war. The carp was eaten by German prisoners!

Bleak pearls

VENICE, LONG unrivalled in the artistic inventiveness and ability of her glass-blowers, conceived among other bright vitreous inventions, the idea of smearing the inside of clear white beads with an opaque pearly varnish; and she executed the device so admirably, and made these deceptive pearls so perfect, that the Government felt called upon to interfere, and formally to prohibit the continuance of a craft by which the public were continually exposed to fraudulent practices.

We know not whether any of these wonderful counterfeits of the sixteenth century are still in existence; if so, their antiquity and connection with the history of pearl-making must render them both curious and valuable.

After a while, the fabrication of false pearls was taken up by a Frenchman named Jacquin, to whom the nacrous idea first occurred, on seeing the water in which bleak had been washed charged with a cloud of minute micaceous particles of this sparkling lymph. He took a small quantity for experiment, and, when the silvery atoms had subsided to the bottom of the vessel, carefully decanted off the water, washed the sediment clean from impurities, and mixing with it a thick, viscid, and colourless fluid, found himself possessed of a beautifully lustrous paste, that he called essence of pearl; with which he went to work, and having formed gypsum beads into the various rounded shapes such as are usually assumed by pearls, he rolled them in the mixture till they were completely coated over with a solid smooth crust.

The Angler's Notebook and Naturalist's Record, 1880

Allis and twaite

RICHARD WALKER, the captor of Britain's most famous carp, Clarissa (which held the UK record for decades) believed that the hardest-fighting UK freshwater fish was the shad. The difficulty in proving this is that they are so rare hardly anyone has ever caught one.

Allis and twaite shads are still found in mostly western British rivers – the Severn and Wye for example – but their numbers have collapsed due to pollution, overfishing (in the past) and habitat damage. Angling for them is now illegal. Shad only enter freshwater to spawn so they are rather like salmon.

Chub for lunch

I NEVER take, or at least keep, a chub under 1lb, and more often, if the fish are running well, not under 1½lb. They are very little use, though on the upper parts of the Thames the people gladly buy them at fourpence a pound, coast fish not often reaching them.

Francis Francis, *A Book on Angling*, 1867

✵

Whitling – a young sea-trout.

Stephen Oliver, *Scenes and Recollections of Fly Fishing*, 1834

Record carp in England up to 1953

25lb 12oz, Dagenham Lake, June 1950, Mr H. J. Grief
25lb 9oz, Dagenham Lake, October 1947, Mr G. Draper
25lb 8oz, Austin's Lake, Clacton, July 1951, Mr R. Sinclair
25lb 0oz, Horsham Lake, July 1951, Mr A. A. Slade
25lb 0oz, Thoresby, August 1952, Mr K. J. Drayton
24lb 12oz, Private Water, West of England, July 1952, Mr M. H. Ingram

The record American carp in 1953 was a fish of 50lb caught by Maurice Vincent on 29 July 1951, in Indiana.

An 83lb 8oz carp was caught in Bon Accord Dam, Pretoria, South Africa, in 1934.

British record fish in 1982

Barbel 13lb 12oz
Bleak 3oz 15 drams
Bream 13lb 8oz
Carp 44lb
Crucian carp 5lb 10oz
Catfish 43lb 8oz
Char 1lb 12oz
Chub 7lb 6oz
Dace 1lb 4oz
Eel 11lb 2oz
Grayling 2lb 13oz
Gudgeon 4oz 4 drams
Perch 4lb 12oz
Pike 40lb
Roach 4lb 1oz
Rudd 4lb 8oz
Salmon 64lb
Tench 10lb 1oz
Trout 19lb 9oz
Rainbow trout 19lb 8oz

Record fish in 2025

Barbel 21lb 2oz
Bleak 4oz 9 drams
Bream 22lb 11oz
Carp 68lb 1oz
Crucian carp 4lb 14oz

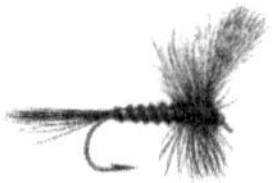

Catfish 150lb 3oz
Char 9lb 8oz
Chub 9lb 5oz
Dace 1lb 5oz
Eel 11lb 3oz
Grayling 4lb 8oz
Gudgeon 5lb
Perch 6lb 3oz
Pike 47lb 5oz
Rudd 4lb 10oz
Salmon 64lb
Tench 15lb 3oz
Trout 31lb 12oz

Only the ruffe and the bullhead records (each just a few ounces) and the salmon record remain unchanged from 1982/83 until 2025. The 64lb salmon famously caught by Miss Ballantine in the 1920s will almost certainly never be bettered.

A selection of sea fish records from 1982/83

Bass 18lb 6oz
Black bream 6lb 14oz
Red bream 9lb 8oz
Coalfish 33lb
Cod 53lb
Skate 226lb
Flounder 5lb 11oz
Halibut 234lb
Ling 57lb
Mackerel 56lb 6oz
Grey mullet 10lb 1oz
Thin-lipped mullet 2lb 9oz

Plaice 10lb 3oz
Pollack 25lb
Blue shark 218lb
Mako shark 500lb
Porbeagle shark 465lb
Tuna 851lb

This is just a selection of sea fish records and although many have drastically increased by the time we reach the 2025 records, there are many exceptions.

The black and red bream records, for example, are unchanged along with the records for dab, flounder, halibut, herring and many others, including all the shark species. Factory ships and overfishing by trawlers have no doubt contributed to the fact that far fewer new records have appeared among the sea fish than among the freshwater fish.

Sixty barbel in one day

NEXT COMES the barbel fisherman: his arrival is previously announced; a punt pole is driven into a certain spot in the river [Thames], where, perhaps, he has had good sport the year before, and the ground is properly baited by one of the resident fishermen of the place, ready for the arrival of his customer.

According to the rule of Thames angling, or rather one of its bye-laws, the fixing a punt-pole in a particular spot, is a sign that the ground is taken, and I never hear of this privilege being disputed. I have known sixty and even eighty barbel taken in one day by a single party in a boat, but this does not happen often in the season. Some of the barbel are of a large size.

The largest which I believe has been taken, weighed fifteen pounds and a half. It was caught by a gentleman of the name of Thompson.

Edward Jesse, *An Angler's Rambles*, 1836

Tar tainted

I HAVE proved by experience that tench are attracted by the smell of tar. On the small lake … I had boats and a punt, the bottoms of which required tarring occasionally. One summer evening, after catching some tench in about ten or twelve feet of water in the afternoon, they went off the feed altogether, and after getting no bites for some time, I went in to dinner, leaving the rod in the punt at the side, with the baits hanging in the water just below the bottom. When I got back I found a tench of about half a pound had taken the worm. I then put the float down almost to the shot, and fished close to the punt, and soon had a much better fish, and they kept on biting until I had to stick a little white feather into the cap of the float to see when I had a bite.

I felt certain then that the tench had been attracted to the spot by the fresh tar, and proved it on other occasions, not invariably, but often enough to feel sure that there was no doubt about it. Since then, whenever I have gone tench fishing, I have bought of a chemist three pennyworth of oil of tar, a perfectly clear liquid like water, with a strong scent of tar. When ground-baiting, I drop two or three drops of this strong spirit on the ground bait and work it in well (it is poison and burns the skin if you carelessly let it dry on). I do not put the spirit on the baits, as it is too strong to please the palate, and kills the worms, but the tench are attracted to the ground bait and soon find the worm or paste.

E. Marston and R. B. Marston, *Fishing for Pleasure and Catching It*, 1906

Angle today

Come, lay by all cares, and hang up all sorrow,
Let's angle today, and ne'er think of tomorrow.

John Dennys, *The Secrets of Angling*, 1613

The rudd – a fish that has considerable popularity among bakers.

H. T. Sheringham, *Fishing: Its Cause, Treatment and Cure*, 1925

*

The tench, the physician among fishes …

Izaak Walton

*

I remember when I was a little boy, I felt a great fish at the end of my line which I drew up almost on the ground, but it dropt in, and the disappointment vexeth me to this very day.

Jonathan Swift, *Letter to Lord Bolingbroke* (1741)

Perch charming

THERE WAS one older man, an excellent fisher and skilled in all kinds of woodcraft, who was pleased to look upon my house as a building erected for the convenience of fishermen; and I was equally pleased when he sat in my doorway to arrange his lines. Once in a while we sat together on the pond, he at one end of the boat, and I at the other; but not many words passed between us, for he had grown deaf in his later years, but he occasionally hummed a psalm, which harmonized well enough with my philosophy.

In warm evenings I frequently sat in the boat playing the flute, and saw the perch, which I seem to have charmed, hovering around me, and the moon travelling over the ribbed bottom, which was strewed with the wrecks of the forest. Formerly I had come to this pond adventurously, from time to time, in dark summer nights, with a companion, and, making a fire close to the water's edge, which we thought attracted the fishes, we caught pouts with a bunch of worms strung on a thread, and when we had done, far in the night, threw the burning brands high into the air like skyrockets, which, coming down into the pond, were quenched with a loud hissing, and we were suddenly groping in total darkness.

Henry David Thoreau, *Walden*, 1845

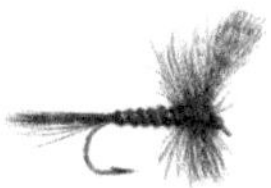

Where they lie

CARP, TENCH, and Eel, seek mud and a still water; Eels under roots or stones, a Carp chooseth the deepest and most still place of pond or river, so does the Tench, and also green weeds, which he likes exceedingly; the greatest Eels love as before; but the smaller ones are found in all sorts of rivers and soils.

Pike, Bream, and Chub, choose sand or clay: the Bream, a gentle stream, and the broadest part of the river; the Pike, still pools full of fry, and shelters himself, the better to surprise his prey unawares, amongst bull-rushes, water-docks, or under-bushes; the Chub loves the same ground, but is more rarely found without some tree to shade and cover him, in large rivers and streams.

Barbel, Roach, Dace, and Ruff, seek gravel and sand more than the Bream, and the deepest parts of the river, where shady trees are more grateful to them, than to the Chub or Chevin.

The Umber seeks marl, clay, clear waters, swift streams, far from the Sea, for I never saw any taken near it; and the greatest plenty of them that I know of, are found in the mountainous parts of Derbyshire, Staffordshire, as Dove Trent, Derwent, &c.

Robert Venables, *The Experienced Angler*, 1662

✵

Let the Angler's apparel be sad dark colours, as sad greys, tawny, purple, hair, or musk colour.

Robert Venables, *The Experienced Angler*, 1662

✵

And ete the olde fishe, and leve the yonge,
Though they moore towgh be uppon the tonge.

Piers of Fulham, 1420

✵

She was used to take delight, with her fair hand
To angle in the Nile, where the glad fish,
As if they knew who 'twas sought to deceive them,
Contended to be taken.

Francis Beaumont and Philip Massinger
(or possibly John Fletcher), *The False One*, 1619

To pluck and hold

FOR THE first and foremost, the cane of which the angle Rod is made, fishers wish not to have big and thick, and yet they need such an one as is tough and strong, for to pluck and hold the fishes, which commonly do mightily fling and struggle when they be caught, but they choose rather that which is small and slimmer, for fear lest if it catch a broad shadow, it might move the doubt and suspicion that is naturally in fishes.

Plutarch, *Moralia*

Sea fish sizes

THE THAMES in central London was still clean enough to fish in the early nineteenth century and shrimp netters operated. The rule stated: shrimps to be sifted through a sieve of three-eighths of an inch between the wires, and those only taken which will not pass through such a sieve. Sea fish were also to be caught: plaice and dabs – extreme length 8in.

Not angling but angling

THE BIGGEST selling non-angling, angling book is *Fly Fishing* by J. R. Hartley. The story began with a TV advertisement for the *Yellow Pages*, a guide older anglers will remember as it was, in pre-internet days, the only way to look up the names, addresses and telephone numbers of businesses and shops and other commercial enterprises.

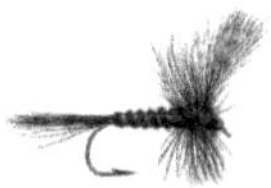

In the advert an elderly man comes home from his local bookshop in despair as they do not have a copy of *Fly Fishing* by J. R. Hartley. His daughter hands him a copy of the *Yellow Pages* and he calls a few bookshops. He finds one that has the book he is looking for, telephones the shop and when the shop owner asks the elderly man his name he replies, 'J. R. Hartley.'

For some reason the advert became a sensation and a 'real' fishing book called *Fly Fishing* by J. R. Hartley was published and became a bestseller. The 'real' book and further books were actually written by author Michael Russell.

Justly or unjustly forgotten angling books?

Practical Dry Fly Fishing, Emlyn Gill, 1912
River Keeper; The Life of William James Lunn, John Waller Hills, 1934
The English Lake District Fisheries, John Watson, 1925
A Fly-fisher's Life, Charles Ritz, 1965
Notes and Reminiscences of My Life as an Angler, William Henderson, 1876

Fishing classics

Dry-Fly Fishing in Theory and Practice, F. M. Halford, 1894
The Way of a Trout with the Fly, G. E. M. Skues, 1921
Tales of Freshwater Fishing, Zane Grey, 1928
Mr Crabtree Goes Fishing, Bernard Venables, 1949
Confessions of a Carp Fisher, BB, 1950

Vanished tackle

THE NOW-VANISHED high street store Woolworths sold fishing tackle up to the mid-1960s under the brand name Winfield. It was of low quality but cheap, which gave many youngsters the chance to try fishing who would otherwise never have been able to start.

Farewell … vanished tackle makers:

- Milbro rods
- Efgeeco bags and other tackle
- Mitchell 300 reels
- East Anglian Rod Company
- The Intrepid Black Prince fixed spool reel
- Illingworth threadline reel
- Wadham pike lures

Vanished tackle makers

MANY REEL makers started life in Redditch which had been famous for its needle making and other metalwork. S. Allcock & Co. made the most famous coarse fishing reel of all: the Aerial centrepin still sought after by enthusiasts and now fetching very high prices.

Other long-gone tackle makers include:

- Reuben Heaton: a Birmingham reel maker
- Dingley, Malloch, Haywood, Bernard
- Onesimus Ustonson: a London reel maker in business from the end of the eighteenth through the early part of the nineteenth century. One or two of their reels were made from solid silver.

Spookfish

THE PACIFIC barreleye – also known sometimes as the spookfish – is the only creature in the world whose eyes are hidden beneath a layer of skin yet still work superbly well. There are several species of barreleye all classified as chimaera. Part of the reason the barreleye still has functioning eyes is that its whole head is transparent.

The fish lives at depths of around 1km and right across the northern Pacific. The barreleye's eyes are very much like binoculars that provide a small but precisely focused view of any bioluminescence – essential because there is no light at the great depths at which the creature lives. The barreleye lives by stealing food trapped by passing jellyfish.

Log-living fish

THE MANGROVE rivulus has a pretty tough life at the best of times. It inhabits slightly saline pools that are in the habit of drying up. To cope with this the rivulus has developed an extraordinary strategy: if its pool vanishes completely the rivulus will wriggle inside a sodden log and in a mangrove swamp there are lots of these. Every crevice of a suitable log will be packed with these fish and, so long as the log remains damp, they can survive for more than two months by which time hopefully the rains have come and the pools have filled up again.

Derivation

THE WORD 'angling' derives from the Old English word 'angol' meaning hook.

*

Giant trevally have learned to catch terns in mid-air by accelerating underwater and then leaping as much as 12ft into the air to catch the birds.

Churchill fishing

WINSTON CHURCHILL, consistently voted the UK's greatest prime minister, is well known as an amateur painter, but few people knew he also enjoyed fishing. In 1949 before attending the first ever Council of Europe Meeting he found time to fish on Lake Garda, and a grainy photograph exists of him fishing with American President Theodore Roosevelt. It was 1943 and Churchill had travelled to the US to discuss the war at the president's rural home in Maryland. They fished a local stream but caught nothing – according to Churchill's memoirs.

Dapping

IN SCOTLAND to this day a favourite method of loch fishing is dapping. A long rod perhaps 16 to 18ft, is set up with the last section of the reel line made from a lightweight material designed to catch the wind. The fly is tied to the end of this and as the fly fisher's boat moves slowly across the water, the long rod ensures the fly can be lifted and then lowered on to the water's surface just as a real fly might land and take off.

In the right conditions the method is deadly because the long rod keeps the fly well away from the boat (thus avoiding scaring the fish) and the fly is constantly in action as no casting is necessary.

Dapping pre-dates the idea of fly casting by centuries – before so-called whipping rods that allowed a fly to be cast any distance, all fly casting was effectively dapping.

Mysterious

EELS ARE one of our most mysterious fish species. We know they swim thousands of miles to the Sargasso Sea off Bermuda to reproduce, but many live and grow for as long as twenty years in UK waters before attempting to migrate. Despite numerous attempts we have never been able to track an eel on its migration from Europe to Bermuda.

Flies for dace

IN VICTORIAN times trout fishermen used to practise by fly fishing for dace on the Lower Thames. Isleworth, which is now part of Greater London, was a very popular place for this but alas the Lower Thames dace have mostly gone. That said, the river is now much cleaner than in the nineteenth century which has resulted in huge numbers of bream dominating the lower tidal Thames.

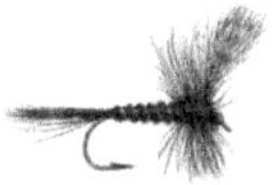

Lungfish

AN AUSTRALIAN lungfish living at the Steinhart Aquarium in San Francisco was genetically tested in 2023 and discovered to be somewhere between 91 and 101 years old.

Lungfish are part of an ancient family that includes the lobe-finned coelacanth. The previous record for longevity was held by Granddad, another lungfish living at an aquarium in China. Lungfish fossils from 100 million years old show that the species has not changed at all in that time, which suggest it was and is supremely adapted to its biological niche.

Wild Trout Trust facts

TROUT SCALES have rings like a tree from which an individual's age can be calculated.

A trout's temperature will always match the temperature of the water in which it lives.

Trout have elliptical eyes which enable them to see approaching food and danger at the same time.

What's a gillie (or ghillie)?

THE WORD gillie (spelt variously as gillie and ghillie) is simply the Scottish Gaelic word for a servant. Ghillies actually help with the fishing by telling anglers which fly to use and where to cast but they also assist with the shooting – specifically stalking red deer in Scotland.

Megamouth

DESPITE ITS size – around 9m long – the megamouth shark was discovered as recently as 1976 and fewer than 300 specimens have been seen since that time (to 2025). The megamouth, like the whale shark, is a filter feeder.

More intelligent – barbel or trout?

STEWART, A firm believer in the principle of imitation of the natural fly, scorned the legion of patterns advocated by the purists. 'Those anglers who think trout will take no fly unless it is an exact imitation of some one of the immense number of flies they are feeding on,' he writes, 'must suppose that they know to a shade the colour of every fly on the water and can detect the least deviation from it – an amount of entomological knowledge that would put to shame the angler himself and a good many naturalists to boot.' Stoddart is equally emphatic.

'I see no reason to suppose that a trout is more intelligent than a chub or a barbel: indeed, from much observation of the latter I definitely place barbel higher in the scale of fish intelligence than trout; and the 5lb chub which inhabit the Kennet are as wary as any fish that swim the rivers of this country. And if chub and barbel will readily eat cherries, cheese, brewers' grains, tallow greaves and other things which they can never possibly have seen before, the belief of many dry-fly men that trout, which eat every living thing that inhabits our rivers, will boggle over the tint of an olive would appear to rest on perilously unstable foundations.'

P. B. M. Allan, *Trout Heresy*, 1936

Baiting for barbel

BAITING A barbel swim is a serious and expensive business, for it involves lobworms, which have a market value of about a penny for ten. It is not much good trying to bait a deep Thames swim with less than a thousand worms, and the enthusiastic barbel fisher uses two or even three thousand before he is satisfied, putting in a thousand on the first evening (either loose or enclosed in balls of clay if the stream is very rapid), five hundred on the second, another five hundred on the third, and so on.

After the swim has been thus fed for several days he expects, small blame to him, to get some return for his trouble and expenditure. He fishes the swim by mooring his punt twenty to thirty yards above it and casting his leger tackle down into it.

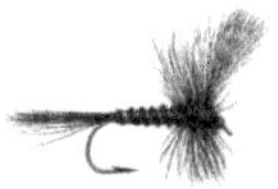

The gut should be fairly stout (the novice's first line and hook will do well enough) and the bait a small lobworm. If the stream is strong, as it usually is in a Thames barbel swim which may be ten feet deep or more, a flat leger lead specially sold for the purpose will hold the bottom better than bullets. A special leger trace with a short length of gimp, on which the lead runs, in the middle of it, is also sold, and it is worth having. A heavy lead frays gut very badly, and the little piece of gimp on the bottom cannot be very visible to the fish, especially as it is at least two and sometimes three feet from the hook.

When he begins to fish the angler may get a bite almost at once, a preliminary to remarkable sport, or he may not get a bite at all. When the fish are really on the feed they are caught in great quantities, a catch of twenty in a day running from three up to seven or eight pounds being nothing uncommon.

A big barbel is a very powerful fighter and gives great though rather solemn sport. The novice should hold it as hard as he dares, but should be ready to let it have line if necessary, taking care never to let it have it slack. The finest battles with barbel fall to the roach fisher, who often in striking at a supposed roach bite hooks a barbel foul.

A fish of five or six pounds so hooked on fine roach tackle will often take half an hour or more in the landing. Barbel fishing as practised from a Thames punt is an easy form of the art, and so far, is to be recommended to the novice. But its expense and uncertainty are not in its favour from the point of view of one who has only a limited amount of time and money to spend on his diversion.

My own experiences with barbel have not been fortunate and I have never had a red-letter day. The nearest approach to it, so far as excitement went, was an occasion when six barbel were safely landed on roach tackle, two of them being hooked in the fin. I once found a dead barbel in the Upper Thames which weighed nearly thirteen pounds, and this would represent about the limit of expectation. I have seen fish in the water which probably exceeded this weight, but anything over ten pounds is a valuable trophy. The Trent barbel are rather smaller as a general rule than the Thames fish, and the biggest of all are probably to be found in the Kennet and Avon.

Eric Parker et al., *Fine Angling for Coarse Fish*, 1921

Favourite haunt

IT WAS the day before Christmas Day, and I was chub fishing under the boughs at the Cherry Orchard above Hampton. I was standing in the stem of my house boat – a home-made one, converted by Bill and myself out of an old dinghy with some matchboard and tarred canvas.

She rowed nearly as lightly as an ordinary boat, and had a little snug stove in her for cooking, etcetera; and I excursioned, fished, and sheltered, and often slept in her too. She was the cheapest investment I ever made. She was pushed into the boughs, which in those days fringed the north bank of the river, and ran out thirty or forty feet into the stream.

It was a favourite haunt of mine in those days, and many a pleasant, lazy, dreamy day have I spent there with a pie and a bottle of sherry, a pipe and a friend, talking over old scenes and memories. It was a capital place to take temporary root in, for the reach was in those days choke-full of fish of all kinds – pike, perch, big trout, barbel, roach, gudgeon, &c. – while the boughs, held huge chub.

I adored the dear old river in those days. It was a whole family to me – an occupation, a history, and almost a religion besides. Now that it has become the prey of the steam-launch demon, the water-works fiend, and the conservancy ogre, its charms have vanished.

Francis Francis, *Reminiscences*, 1887

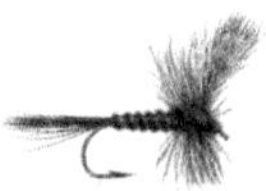

Chapter 8

FACTS AND FANCIES

THE BRITISH record char as of 2025 was caught in Loch Arkaig by W. Fairburn. It weighed 9lb 8oz.

✵

The oldest fishing club in the UK is the Amwell Magna Fishery. The club controls Izaak Walton's favourite stretch of the River Lea in Hertfordshire. It was founded in 1831. The Houghton Club on the River Test is older but there is a gap in their tenure on the Test.

✵

There are estimated to be 2,300 angling clubs in the UK.

✵

As of 2025 there were reckoned to be roughly 2 million anglers in the UK, but that figure included many who fished only very infrequently.

✵

There were an estimated 753,000 sea anglers in Britain as of 2025.

Loch Tay monsters

I KNOW no salmon fishery in the world that habitually yields such large fish as Loch Tay. The average of fish caught in Loch Tay for some years has been something like 22lb; a fish under 20lb is said to be rather exceptional.

Week after week, each season, have we seen the returns with 25, 27, 30, and 35-pounders plentifully present, and at last this year a 60-pounder was brought to land upon a single gut.

Francis Francis *Reminiscences*, 1887

*

No angler can be a good man.

Lord Byron, *Don Juan*, 1824

*

Pound for pound [the barbel] is a much more powerful fish than a trout.

P. B. M. Allan, *Trout Heresy*, 1936

Do soles spring from prawns?

WITH REGARD to the origin of soles, the strange position has been advanced that they spring from prawns; to prove the correctness of this absurdity, a noted French free-thinker having produced a supply, kept them in sea-water, and obtained, in due time, a handsome fry of young soles, begotten, as he gave out and believed, in the body of these crustaceans.

Assuming the fact to have been correctly reported, the natural explanation would be, that the eggs of the sole, which are viscid, and readily attach themselves to different bodies, happening to do so in this instance to prawns, were hatched on their persons, as they would, under favourable conditions, have been anywhere else without any help from these shell-fish.

The Angler's Notebook and Naturalist's Record, 1880

A proverb at Winchester

TO BE a perfect trout fisher, to my mind, a man should follow no other branch of fishing. It spoils his hand if he does. I myself, from the practice of striking so hard in both salmon, pike, and other fishing, used to lose numbers of fish and flies in the course of the season; and what made it the more vexing was that they were nearly always the best and heaviest fish. At Winchester they used to have a sort of proverb about me.

'Why, he loses more fish than any man in Winchester, John,' said a severe critic one day to old John Hammond, that most artful old provider of fishing requisites.

'What did you say, sir?' said John, putting his hand up to his ear, for he very often couldn't hear anything he did not want to. The criticism was repeated. 'Ah,' said the sly old being, with a couple of nods of the head, and two taps on the lid of his snuff-box, 'but then he hooks more!'

After which a very bad fit of deafness came over him for a minute or two, till a little boy came in for a 'penny hook and a withy', and turned the conversation. Since that time, however, I have done less coarse fishing, devoting my attention to the grayling when the time for coarse fish comes on, and the result has been most striking. I now lose less fish than many of the single-hand rod men.

When you are given to too heavy striking, the best provision you can adopt is to lighten your rod and tackle: have a lighter or more flexible rod, and a lighter line.

Francis Francis, *A Book on Angling*, 1867

Dapping roach

ROACH WILL not unfrequently take the artificial fly, especially when first scouring themselves after spawning; and during the last few years I have caught some very fine specimens when dapping for Chub with the imitation grasshopper.

H. T. Sheringham, *Elements of Angling*, 1930

Poetic

And through their Rockes with crooked winding way,
Thy mother Avon runnest soft to seeke:
In whose fayre streames the speckled Trout doth play,
The Roche, the Dace, the Gudgin and the Bleeke
Teach me the skill with slender Line and Hooke
To take each Fish of River, Pond, and Brooke.

John Dennys, *The Secrets of Angling*, 1613

When carp arrived

THE WORD carpa, whatever its origin may be, is a very old one, occurring first in Cassiodorus, a writer of the sixth century; long after whom, we find the words carpera and carpo used as designations for this fish by writers of the thirteenth century: the latter occurs in a legend of Cæsarius, quoted by Beckmann, where the Prince of Evil, indulging in a frolic, appears in a coat of mail, having 'scales like a carpo'?

The English form of the word does not occur in the *Anglo-Saxon Dictionary* of Alfric Archbishop of York, who died in 1051, but is used in Dame Berners' book on Angling, published in 1486, wherein 'carpe' is declared to be 'a daynteous fysshe, but there ben but few in Englonde, and therefore I wryte the lesse of hym. He is an evyll fysshe to take, for he is so stronge enarmyd in the mouthe that there maye noo weke harnays hold hym?'

The usually assigned period for their introduction into our country, by Leonard Mascal, of Plumstead (Sussex), in the reign of Henry the Eighth, must consequently be erroneous.

The precise dates when carp were severally transported into France, Prussia, Sweden, and Denmark, and from what aboriginal stock all these different colonists sprang, are points not easily determined; as, however, they appear to thrive most in warm latitudes, and are found to dwindle remarkably in the north, the supposition of their having a southern origin is by no means improbable.

Hardy and prolific beyond most other fish, their spread, when once mankind had begun to naturalize them, was most rapid; and towards the middle of the sixteenth century there was scarce a country unacquainted with carp; in many, stews on a vast scale were stocked exclusively with cyprini, and thus an unfailing supply of orthodox diet for Lent and meagre-days was never wanting in larder or pond.

About this time, the Reformation having prepared the way for our emancipation from an enforced diet, and carp being left like other fish to stand or fall according to its deserts, and proving, so tried, anything but first-rate either as regards digestibility or flavour, soon became scarce in the market, and was never seen at a feast.

Charles Badham, *Fish Tattle*, 1854

Grayling

THERE ARE fourteen species of grayling, including the Arctic grayling, European grayling, Baikal black grayling, Baikal white grayling and the Mongolian grayling, to name just a few.

Minnows

ALL MINNOWS are members of the carp family. They are known in Ireland as pinkeens.

Types of minnows

- Bluntnose
- Common shiner
- Common emerald shiner
- Cheat
- Cutlips
- Desert
- Eurasian
- Fathead
- Loach minnow

- Ozark
- Pikeminnow
- Pug nose minnow
- Silverhawk
- Long jaw
- Suckermouth
- White Cloud Mountain minnow

Almost the oldest

THE HOUGHTON Fishing Club is the world's oldest, but not the world's oldest and most continuous. It was founded in 1822. Rather than rent their twenty miles of the River Test below Stockbridge the club very sensibly bought the freehold.

The club is also the most secretive fishing club in the world. It cannot be contacted via the internet or phone; only the members and riverkeepers know who the other members are; you cannot apply to be a member but must be put forward by another member.

Membership was originally limited to just thirteen anglers, although numbers have crept up to twenty-five. Most of the members were either at Eton or Harrow and most are the sons of titled landowners. The club employed three generations of the Lunn family as gillies and riverkeepers. A Lunn was working for the club in the 1860s and his great-grandson was still working for the club in the 1980s.

✵

The earliest depiction of an angler is on the walls of a 3,000-year-old tomb at Thebes in Egypt.

✵

The oldest fishing book in English was written by Dame Juliana Berners (1388–1460). *A Treatyse of Fysshynge Wyth an Angle* is first mentioned in 1496.

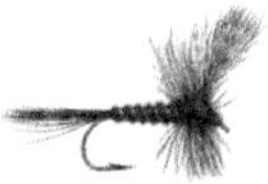

Greedy biters

ALL ANGLERS know that gobies are very greedy biters; in allusion to which Shakespeare, prince of poets, says:

> But fish not with this melancholy bait,
> For this fool's gudgeon, this opinion.

And another sings –

> What gudgeons are we men,
> Every woman's easy prey!
> Though we've felt the hook, again
> We bite, and they betray.

Charles Badham, *Fish Tattle*, 1854

A tench on the temples

TENCH, LIKE the gudgeon, is held a dish for invalids, and has been pressed into their service in more ways than one: for convalescents who are not yet allowed mutton, may safely go from gruel and sago to tench broth; and in febrile attacks, it used to be applied to the palms of the feet and hands, to absorb the fever; laid over the region of the liver in jaundice, still more wonderful results ensued. After one or two applications the skin of the … patient would, we are assured, return to a perfectly natural colour, whilst the fish became more and more saffron in hue, and at length expired in a jaundice; on being cut open it was found dyed throughout of a deep gamboge yellow!

A live tench applied to the temple has been … known to assuage the throbbings of nervous headaches; and worn round the neck, to cure sore eyes: it was also found equally potent in obstinate worm cases.

Charles Badham, *Fish Tattle*, 1854

✵

Give me mine angle, we'll to the river: there,
My music playing far off, I will betray
Tawny finn'd fishes; my bended hook shall pierce
Their slimy jaws, and as I draw them up,
I'll think them every one an Antony,
And say 'Ah, ha! you're caught.

Shakespeare, *Antony and Cleopatra*

Bleak prospect

MOST FISHERMEN will have, on occasions, remarked Bleak swimming round and round in circles with their heads above the surface of the water, as if suffering from vertigo.

These gyrations are caused by thin white tapeworms, sometimes as much as 9 or 10 inches long and three-tenths of an inch wide, which get into the intestines of the fish.

H. T. Sheringham, *Elements of Angling*, 1930

Fleas like a loach

IZAAK WALTON says that the loach 'groweth not to be above a finger long, and is no thicker than is suitable to that length,' but then he adds, it is '… a dainty dish at table'.

We must, however, discriminate a little here, for there are three distinct species, of very different merits: 'he that feedeth and is bred in little and clear swift brooks or rills, over gravel, and in the sharpest streams, is the best; inferior to them in quality and size, though from the same locality, is the C. *tænia*, characterized by a forked prickle in front of the eyes: and lastly, there is the common pond loach.'

The fecundity of the loach is immense; they begin to propagate very young, and seem to be always either spawning or in roe: this surprising power of reproduction was sufficiently known to be proverbial in Shakespeare's day.

In a dialogue between two Rochester carriers, he makes one of these say to his companion, 'Your chimney lie breeds fleas like a loach.'

Charles Badham, *Fish Tattle*, 1854

Cane rods

THE BUILT cane rod which superseded whole cane, greenheart, hickory, lancewood and Spanish reed, was not invented in England (contrary to widespread belief) nor was it first made by the famous Northumbrian tackle makers Hardy Bros.

In fact, the built cane rod – six precisely planed and tapered sections of solid bamboo glued together to create a rod with a hexagonal cross section – was the brainchild of Samuel Phillipe, from Easton, Pennsylvania, in the United States.

Though few are now made, built cane still has enormous appeal – if you are fishing in a beautiful, natural environment why would you choose to use a rod made in a vast hi-tech factory using highly unnatural materials such as boron or carbon fibre? Instead, you can choose a natural material, cane, which seems a better fit in a world of rivers and streams, woods and meadows.

Birds and otters

THE FACT that cormorants are trained to fish for their human masters in China is well known. Less well known is the fact that otters were once trained to fish across much of Asia and in parts of Europe.

They were attached to a line which was then attached to a harness on the otter's back. The otter would then chase or herd fish into the fisherman's net.

✵

In shape the bream bears a marked resemblance to a pair of bellows …

Eric Parker et al., *Fine Angling for Coarse Fish*, 1929

Roach bites

1. The Hesitant – a half-hearted flicker repeated at intervals.
2. The Touch – a quick slight movement. More often than not one is caught napping.
3. The Pluck – the float dives down in a flash.

Edward Ensom, *The Roach*, 1953

List of the Deeps on the Thames

Chertsey, 200 yards, being from the weir eastward.

Weybridge, 800 yards, being from the weir down to Holliday's Bay.

Shepperton, 200 yards, being called the lower deep, and eastward of the drain.

Sunbury, 100 yards, being from the weir eastward.

Thames Ditton, 250 yards, being from Keen's wharf northward.

Staines, 140 yards, being from 60 yards westwards to 80 yards eastward of the bridge.

Penton Hook, 200 yards, being on the west side of the hook.

Chertsey, 140 yards, being from 60 yards westward to 80 yards eastward of the bridge.

Shepperton, 200 yards, being called the upper deep, and situated to the eastward.

Shepperton, 240 yards, being called the old deep, and eastward of the creek rails.

Walton, 100 yards, being westward of the horse bridge, and called the Walton Sale.

Walton, 150 yards, being at the Earl of Tankerville's.

Sunbury, 100 yards, being opposite the church.

Hampton, 350 yards, being from the west angle of the church steeple to the west side of H. Hase's, Esq.

Hampton Court, 200 yards, being from the summerhouse of the palace to the eastward.

Thames Ditton, 512 yards, being at Lord Henry Fitzgerald's.

Kingston, 40 yards, being eastward of the river which runs from Ewell.

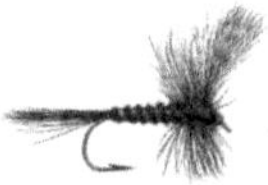

Kingston, 60 yards, being from 30 yards westward to 30 yards eastward of the bridge.
Twickenham, 150 yards, being at the house of Sir W. Waller, Bart.
Richmond, 700 yards, being westward of the bridge to the Duke of Buccleuch's.
Fulham, 50 yards, being from 30 yards westward to 20 yards eastward of the bridge.
Battersea, 20 yards, being from 10 yards westward to 10 yards eastward of the bridge.

Huge haul

IN 1911, Mr R. Graham caught the following large perch in one session on a Derbyshire pond: 4lb 13 and a quarter ounces; 4lb 12 ounces; 4lb 6 ounces; 3lb 13 ounces; 3lb 11 ounces.

Where to Fish, 1911

Barbel shoal

ONCE DURING frosty weather, when the water was like glass, we – John Keene, one of the best-known professionals, was with me – saw, deep down in a hole in the river below Old Windsor weir, a shoal of barbel which must have numbered nearly a hundred, lying in a kind of massed formation, one lot above the other. They refused to have anything to do with worms and bread-crust, and scarcely moved when the punt-pole was quietly lowered into their midst.

A. R. Matthews, *Freshwater Fishing*, 1922

Stewed trout

FOR YOUR stewed Trouts, you must cut them on the side, as for broiling: there are divers wayes of stewing; the English hath one way, the French hath another way, the Italian hath another way: I may speak this; for I have been admitted into the Kitchins, to furnish men of most Nations, when they have been in England.

We will begin with the English: He broyleth first upon a Charcoale fire; the first thing that you must have a care of is, when your Grid-iron is hot you must coole it with ruff Suet, then the skin of your Fish will not break, with care of turning them: when they are nigh broyled, take them off the Grid-iron; set on a Chafing-dish of coals in a Stew-pan, or Dish; put in a good quantity of fresh Butter, so much Vinegar as will give the relish, a penny-worth of beaten Cinamon; then put in your broyled fish, and let them stew, about halfe an houre will be sufficient, being turned: adorn your Dish with Sippets, take the fish out of the stew-pan, lay them for the service, be sure to squease a Lemmon on them: I will warrant them good victuall.

The Italian he stewes upon a Chafing-dish of coals, with white Wine, Cloves, and Mace, Nutmegs sliced, a little Ginger: you must understand when this fish is stewed, the same liquor that the fish is stewed in, must be beaten with some Butter and the juyce of a Lemmon, before it is dish'd for the service. The French doe add to this a slice or two of Bacon.

Thomas Barker, *The Art of Angling*, 1651

My hand alone my work can do
So I can fish and study too.

William Basse, published in his friend Izaak Walton's *The Compleat Angler*, 1653

Hazel rods

SUCH WHO most commend the hazel-rod, (which I also value and praise, but for different reasons), above the cane; do it because, say they, the slender rod saveth the line; but my opinion is, that the equal bending of the rod chiefly, next to the skill of the Angler, saveth the line, and the slenderness I conceive principally serveth to make the

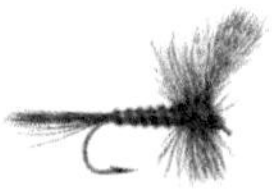

fly-rod long and light, easy to be managed with one hand, and casteth the fly far, which are to me the considerations chiefly to be regarded in a fly-rod.

Robert Venables, *The Experienced Angler*, 1662

✵

Razorfish and sea horses are the only fish that swim while remaining vertical in the water.

Pike song

He, knowing it a fish of stubborn sway,
Puls up his rod, but soft: (as having skill)
Wherewith the hooke fast holds the fishe's gill.
Then all his line he freely yeeldeth him,
Whilst furiously all up and downe doth swimme
Th' insnared fish ...
By this the pike, cleane wearied, underneath
A willow lyes and pants (if fishes breathe):
Wherewith the fisher gently puls him to him,
And, least his haste might happen to undo him,
Lays down his rod, then takes his line in hand,
And by degrees getting the fish to land,
Walkes to another poole."

William Browne, *Britannia's Pastorals* (Fifth Song), 1613

Homeric fish

IN THE *Iliad* and *Odyssey* no fish appear at banquets or in the houses of the well-to-do: only in connection with the poorest or starving do they obtain mention.

William Radcliffe, *Fishing from the Earliest Times*, 1921

Trout and noise

IT GOES against the grain to differ with such a charmful and themeful author as Sir Herbert Maxwell. But his conclusion that fish in Loch Ken were disturbed every time a shooting party half to three-quarters of a mile away discharged their guns cannot be reconciled with the experiments made by me in July 1918 to test the behaviour of trout, when guns were fired, not half a mile away, but quite close to them.

Three of us, all accustomed to watching fish, selected a narrow shallow burn in which the trout ran from fingerlings up to fish three or four years old. Each in turn fired the gun (an ordinary 12 bore shotgun), with the usual shooting charge of powder and No. 5 shot. At the first two trials only was the shot extracted, so as to eliminate any vibration set up by its striking the opposite bank. Two of us lying hidden in the grass observed from different spots.

The gun was fired eight feet, four feet, and three feet above the surface of the stream, which varied in breadth from eight to ten feet, and in depth from sixteen to nineteen inches. It was fired into the air and into the opposite bank (struck from four to two feet above the water) in a direct line above different fishes, lying either singly or in shoals from five to nine inches from the bottom in small pools or runs sixteen to nineteen inches deep. Care was taken to fire upstream, to prevent the trout being startled by the flash of the cartridge.

In no case did the trout take the very least notice, or give any sign of having heard the explosion or felt the concussion of the shot on the opposite bank, composed on three occasions of alluvial soil and on two of rock. Never once did a fish move or go down: in fact, in one of the experiments over a single well-grown trout, the fish was rising again to the natural fly in less than thirty seconds after the discharge of the gun.

William Radcliffe, *Fishing from the Earliest Times*, 1921

Handsome but coarse

IN THE Thames and part of the river Lea there are many, very fine and large barbel: I knew of one taken at Shepperton, weighing nineteen pounds ten ounces; they are a very handsome Fish, but their flesh is coarse,

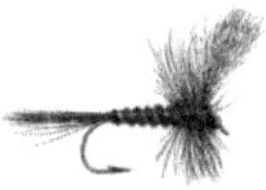

and therefore considered but of little value for the table; yet I have been told, by several persons, that they eat very well, especially when baked, with veal stuffing in their belly, as do the smaller ones split and fried in batter, or with slices of pickled pork or bacon; but the spawn of Barbel is not fit for food, as it generally acts as a strong cathartic, and frequently as an emetic.

The Barbel is prized for being a game Fish, affording excellent sport to the Angler, mixed with some labour and much anxiety: for when of a large size, they are exceedingly crafty, sulky, and strong, struggling a long time after they are hooked, often lying motionless at the bottom for some minutes, then running under banks, or shelves, into large beds of weeds, in fact, trying every possible way to get off the hook, or break your line, which they certainly will effect if you are deficient in skill, or your tackle is in any respect faulty.

Thomas Salter, *The Art of Angling*, 1833

Old baits – a list

- Cows' brains
- Tares
- Elderberries
- Silkweed
- Hemp
- Bees
- Daddy-long-legs
- Barley
- Slugs
- Frogs
- Bacon
- Greaves

Wagtail trust

I WELL remember once how a grey-wagtail trusted me.

The stream was in spate; shallow, pool, and fall were lost in one great tearing yellow torrent. All other sounds were drowned and quiet converse with my companion was impossible, so we lunched in silence on a great grey granite rock round which the mass of seething, raging water pressed.

Presently a wagtail, chasing gnats from stone to stone, came up the stream, silently, for the low sound of her wings could not be heard in the water's din. Up and up she came, surely she must visit our rock! 'Keep as still as a statue,' I signed to my companion. As silently as a butterfly she alighted near me. Now she ran behind my back after a gnat, now she flitted across my thighs and, sitting on my boot for a moment, wagged her tail, her fragile foot on my seeming-great shapeless one.

W. C. Stewart, *The Practical Angler*, 1867

Fish or no fish

ANGLING, WHEN once embarked in by any person possessed of a reasonable amount of soul and brains, becomes a passion, and like other passions will grow and feed upon the smallest possible amount of encouragement. Fish or no fish, whenever opportunity offers, the angler may be found at the waterside.

If this only went on in fine weather, people could understand it, but now-a-days, even in summer, the weather is not always fine; and when a man is seen standing in the water for hours in a torrent of rain, with benumbed hands and an empty basket, doubts of the individual's sanity naturally suggest themselves, mixed with feelings of pity for the terrible consequences in the way of colds, rheumatism, &c., which it is supposed must inevitably follow, but rarely does.

W. C. Stewart, *The Practical Angler*, 1867

Etonians fishing

IN HIS long-forgotten book *An Incompleat Angler*, published in 1976, Lord Hardinge of Penshurst recalled a journey to Iceland made during the war aboard HMS *King George VI* on which he was serving. He noticed on a map of the area around the Icelandic capital Reykjavik that there was a fine-looking stream nine miles from the city.

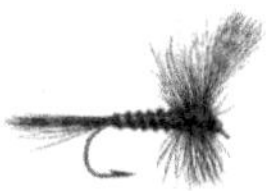

He and the other officers were given four hours' leave when they arrived at Reykjavik leaving for their shore leave at 2 p.m. They were given strict instructions to be back on the ship by 6 p.m.

Hardinge was such a fanatic that he calculated that by running, jogging and fast walking he could cover the nine miles, fish for half an hour and just about get back by 6 p.m. Astonishingly he managed it. In the thirty minutes he spent fishing, he even managed a 2½lb sea trout.

Lord Hardinge writes as if he were still living before the Great War. He and his friends seem quite regularly to have been invited to fish and picnic with the royal family at Balmoral and he is never really surprised to bump into fellow old Etonians picnicking and fishing alongside him.

English chalk streams

Adur, Sussex
Avon, Hampshire
Stour, Dorset
Banwell, Somerset
Bulbourne, Hertfordshire
Chess, The Chilterns
Dour, Kent. Known for its high water quality.
Gade, The Chilterns
Itchen, Hampshire
Kennet, Berkshire. Known for its fly fishing.
Mimram, The Chilterns. Known for its biodiversity.
Misbourne, The Chilterns
Test, Hampshire
Ver, Hertfordshire. Known for its pure alkaline waters and unique flora and fauna.
Wylye, Wiltshire

Quotations from Izaak Walton

I have laid aside business and gone a fishing.

Angling may be said to be so like the mathematics that it can never be fully learned.

No life is so happy and so pleasant as the life of the well-govern'd angler.

God never did make a more calm, quiet, innocent recreation than angling.

Rivers and the inhabitants of the watery element were made for wise men to contemplate, and fools to pass by without consideration.

Dog-skin sandpaper

DOGFISH SKIN was used by furniture makers to smooth timber in the days before commercial sandpaper became available.

Goodbye line dryers

LINE DRYERS were once essential for fly fishers. After a day's fishing the angler's silk fly line had to be carefully wound off the reel and onto what looked like a small spinning wheel – as it turned the line was laid across an open-work frame so that no section of the line lay on top of any other section – the idea was to dry the line quickly before it became mouldy and began to rot. With the advent of plastic fly lines tens of thousands of line dryers became obsolete overnight.

Leventon's Editor

SANDY LEVENTON, former editor of *Trout & Salmon* magazine, invented The Editor, a salmon fly that has become one of the most successful new flies in more than a century.

Fish nicknames

Lady of the stream – grayling
The doctor fish – tench

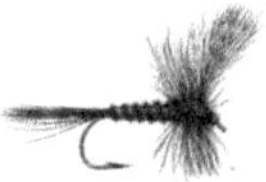

Dustbin lid – large common bream
Rubber lips – chub
Alderman – chub
Redfin – roach
Poor man's trout – dace

Wild numbers

BETWEEN 1,100 and 2,200 billion wild fish are estimated to have been caught by trawlers from 2000–2012. That's between 74 and 83 million tonnes of fish each year. The figures were published by Cambridge University in 2024.

Pulitzer fishing

ONLY ONE fishing book has ever won the Pulitzer, America's most prestigious literary prize. The book is *The Old Man and the Sea* by Ernest Hemingway published in 1952.

Amphibious fish

MUD SKIPPERS – a member of the twenty-three-strong goby family – can live for long periods in and out of water. They are amphibious fish that have intrigued scientists because their pectoral fins are positioned underneath their bodies and they are jointed like limbs. They are considered a living example of the kind of fish that first moved from the water to land.

Flounder stamping

FLOUNDER STAMPING was once common on the wide sandy estuaries of lowland Scotland and England. You walk barefoot across the sand at low tide until you feel a slight wriggle under your feet – you then use your spear to catch the fish taking care not to spear your own feet!

Types of Salmon

- Coho
- Chinook
- Pink
- Chum
- Sockeye
- Atlantic

Types of fishing knots

Palomar – good for braided line and tying on hooks.
Blood knot – good for tying on eyed hooks and joining two pieces of line.
Uni knot – good for joining two pieces of line.
Clinch – good for flies and lures.
FG – for braided lines.
The oldest angler's knot is probably the turtle – used for tying artificial flies to fly line.

Rivers in Wales with salmon runs

Llifon, Carrog, Ogwen, Seiont, Llynfi, Erch, Dwyfor, Glaslyn, Mawddach, Dyfi, and Dwyryd.

Cast or leader

MORE TRADITIONALLY known as a cast, a leader is a thin length of nylon usually around 9ft–12ft long, to which the game fisherman ties his fly at one end. At the other end the leader is tied to the thick plastic or silk casting line. Some anglers swear by tapered leaders; others simply use a short stretch of standard monofilament.

Wet-fly anglers in the north of England traditionally have three or even four droppers on the leader (or cast). Great skill is needed when casting four flies to avoid tangles.

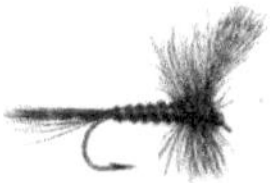

Rivers in Scotland with salmon runs

Spey, Tay, Dee, Tweed, Teeth, Earn, North and South Esk, Lossie, Nairn, Deveron, Findhorn, Don, Shin, Connon and Helmsdale.

Longest rivers in Scotland

Tay – 120 miles (193km)
Spey – 107 miles (172km)
Clyde – 106 miles (171km)
Tweed – 97 miles (156km)
Dee – 85 miles (137km)
Don – 82 miles (132km)
Nath – 71 miles (112km)
Forth – 65 miles (105km)
Findhorn – 63 miles (101km)
Deveron – 61 miles (98km)

Trout eggs

A BROWN trout will produce 900 eggs per pound of its weight.

Record catch

THE *Guinness Book of Angling* lists the record for the greatest number of separate species of fish caught by one angler in a year; he landed at least one fish each of eighty-five species!

Most valuable angling book

A FIRST edition of Izaak Walton's *The Compleat Angler* would cost at least £75,000. It's the most valuable angling book ever published.

First edition

A FIRST edition of *The Old Man and the Sea* by Ernest Hemingway cost around £19,000 in 2024.

Floats traditional

FLOATS WERE traditionally made from bird quills. Goose quills and crow quills were very popular and to make them carry more shot for faster or deeper water, a simple cork body was added.

Wild rainbow

THE RIVER Wye in Derbyshire is one of only a tiny handful of rivers in the UK that has a wild breeding population of rainbow trout.

Notorious bleak

BLEAK ACHIEVED some notoriety at the International Festival Angling Championship Match, fished on the Thames, between Reading and Goring, on August 25, 1951. Teams (twelve anglers in each) from France, Belgium, Holland and Germany took part, and in all there were six hundred competitors. Bleak in their thousands were captured.

Birmingham AA were easy winners with 72lb 12¾oz, of mostly bleak; Coventry were runners-up with 47lb 5oz. Individual winner was Mr R. Kay, of the Birmingham AA, with 17½lb (all bleak, bar two dace).

Altogether 987lb 15oz of Thames bleak were weighed in and returned to water.

Faddist, *Memorable Coarse Fish*, 1953

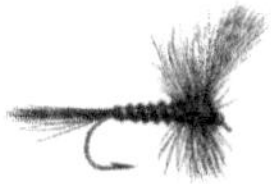

Fishing books

DEWAR'S *South Country Trout Streams* is an interesting and useful little book, though the rivers of which it treats are not as a rule likely to prove a happy fishing ground for the ordinary man, being, as has been said, things of price.

Exmoor Streams, by C. F. Wade, gives a good idea of the fishing to be obtained in that delectable part of the country. Mr F. H. Amphlett's *The Thames, Where to Fish it and How*, is a useful guide to the Metropolitan River.

The volumes on Wales in the *Highways and Byways* series from the pen of that good angler Mr A. G. Bradley are enriched with a good deal of fishing information happily conveyed.

Mr P. Geen's *What I Have Seen While Fishing* also gives some topographical information both about Scotland and Ireland. There are valuable pages also in the books of the late Mr J. W. Martin ('The Trent Otter') describing reaches of the Ouse, Trent, and other East Anglian waters, and there is a good deal of detached information scattered about in the angling library generally.

A word of caution, however, with regard to fishing guide books and literature is not out of place. However accurate the information in a book or article is at the date of its publication, it does not follow that it will be accurate five, or even two, years later. Change is a melancholy but insidious thing, and conditions are apt to alter materially from lustre to lustre. Therefore, before staking a holiday on the faith of a printed page, an angler will always do well to make inquiry as to the permanence of the conditions of which he has read.

T. C. Hofland, *The British Angler's Manual*, 1839

Stickleback battles

THE STICKLEBACK is certainly its knight-errant: now, with sheathed weapons and glittering in green and purple, he tenderly woos the object of his devotion, or armed cap-à-pie patrols a watchful sentinel before her nuptial bower; now he fiercely disputes with rival claimants the possession of a favourite nook, or bristling with spines charges through the liquid plains in search of other Sticklebacks as pugnacious and more penetrable than himself.

The movements of Sticklebacks in confinement are described by those who have watched them as being most warlike. When a few are first turned in, they swim about in a shoal, apparently exploring their new habitation.

Suddenly one will take possession of a particular corner of the tub, or, as it will sometimes happen, of the bottom, and will instantly commence an attack on his companions; and if either of them ventures to oppose his sway, a regular and furious battle ensues: the two combatants swim round and round each other with the greatest rapidity, biting and endeavouring to pierce each other with their spines, which on these occasions are projected. Contests of this sort frequently last several minutes before either will give way; and when one does submit, imagination can hardly conceive the vindictive fury of the conqueror.

H. Cholmondeley-Pennell, *The Angler Naturalist*, 1875

Minnow magic

ON CROSSING a brook, I saw from the foot-bridge something at the bottom of the water which had the appearance of a flower. Observing it attentively, I found that it consisted of a circular assemblage of Minnows. Their heads all met in a centre; and their tails diverging at equal distances and being elevated above their heads, gave them the appearance of a flower half-blown. One was larger than the rest; and as often as a straggler came in sight, he quitted his place to pursue him, and, having driven him away, returned to it again no other Minnow offering to take it in his absence. This I saw him do several times. The object that had been attracting them all was a dead Minnow, which they seemed to be devouring.

J. C. Loudon, *Magazine of Natural History*, 1824

When pike were rare

DR YARRELL bases his opinion upon the great rarity of Pike in former times in England, which he proves thus: 'That Pike were rare formerly may be inferred from the fact that, in the latter part of the thirteenth century, Edward I, who condescended to regulate the prices of the different sorts of fish then brought to market, ... fixed the value of Pike higher than that of fresh Salmon, and more than ten times greater than that of the best Turbot or Cod.

'In proof of the estimation in which Pike were held in the reign of Edward III, I may refer to the lines of Chaucer –

> Full many a fair part rich hade he in mewe,
> And many a breme, and many a Luce [pike] in stewe.'

Pike are mentioned in an Act of the 6th year of the reign of Richard II (1382), which relates to the forestalling of fish. Pike were dressed in the year 1461 at the great feast given by George Nevil, Archbishop of York. ... Pike were so rare in the reign of Henry VIII, that a large one sold for double the price of a house-lamb in February; and a Pickerel, or small Pike, for more than a fat capon.

Thomas Stoddart, *Angler's Companion*, 1892

Chapter 9

WEIGHTS AND MEASURES

Thames size restrictions in the early nineteenth century

NO FISH of the species hereinafter mentioned shall be taken in or out of the River Thames, or having been taken, shall be had in possession, or exposed for sale on the River Thames, or on the shore thereof, or on any lands adjoining or near to the river, of less than the respective sizes and dimensions following. (This section is not intended to apply to any person who takes such fish accidentally, and forthwith returns the same to the water with the least possible injury.)

Pike or jack – extreme length 18in
Bream – extreme length 10in
Perch – extreme length 8in
Chub – extreme length 10in
Roach – extreme length 7in
Dace – 6in
Barbel – 13in
Trout – 16in

Grayling – 9in
Carp – 10in
Tench – 8in
Rudd – 6in
Gudgeon – 4in
Flounders – 7in
Smelt – 5½in
Soles – extreme length 7in

At this period the close season was known as the fence season.

Name that carp

CARP CAUGHT many times become famous and even end up with individual names. Mary was caught and recaught for many years at Wraysbury Pits. Other famous carp include The Bishop, The Black Mirror, Heather the Leather, and Basil.

Conviction for forestalment of lampreys in the reign of Edward II

HUGH MATFREY, fishmonger of London, was attached to answer our Lord the King, and the Mayor of London, because that he, the same Hugh, on the Monday next after the Feast of Annunciation of Saint Mary [25 March] in the 4th year of the reign of King Edward, bought of Thomas Lespicer, of Portesmuth, six pots of lampreys of Nauntes, which the said Thomas had brought to London on the preceding Saturday, and stowed away in the house of the same Hugh, against the customs and ordinances used in the City; seeing that he ought to have exposed the same for sale immediately after his arrival, under the wall of St Margaret's Church in Bridge Street, and there to have stood for the purpose of selling such lampreys, the next four days after his arrival; in such manner as is contained in a certain Black Book of Memoranda of the time of Gregory de Rokesle, formerly Mayor:

whereas he, the said Hugh, bought the said lampreys on the second day after their arrival, and that in his house, against the customs and ordinances aforesaid, in forestalment, and to the no small damage, of the good men in the City dwelling. And he was asked how he would acquit himself thereof.

Whereupon, he appeared, and said he was guilty thereof, and he put himself upon the favour of the Mayor as to the same. And the said Mayor, with the assent and will of the Aldermen, and at the instance of Sir John Devery, wholly forgave the said Hugh, as well as the said Thomas, the trespass aforesaid.

And the said Thomas, touching the holy relics, made oath that in future, when he should happen to come with lampreys to the City, whether his own or belonging to other persons, he would not sell them elsewhere than at the place appointed, and according to the ordinance aforesaid. And the aforesaid Hugh in like manner made oath that in future he would warn, or would cause to be warned, all foreign dealers bringing lampreys to the City, that they must expose them for sale in the place appointed, and according to the ordinance aforesaid; and that in future he would not buy any lampreys of them, against the ordinance aforesaid: and further, that in future he would not shew contempt for the Mayor or Aldermen by any unbecoming words, or in any other way; under a penalty of 10 pounds, to the Chamber of Guildhall to be paid, in case he should be convicted thereof.

Henry Riley (tr.), *Memorials of London and London Life in the 13th, 14th and 15th Centuries*, 1868

Thames record carp

AS OF 2025, Nick Helleur held the record for the biggest carp ever caught from the Thames. It was a mirror weighing 50lb 12oz.

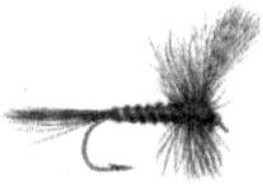

Legendary fish

IN THE year 1497 a giant Jack-killer – a pike – was apparently captured in the vicinity of Mannheim, with the following announcement in Greek appended to his muzzle: 'I am the first fish that was put into this pond by the hands of the Emperor Frederic the Second, on this third day of October, 1262.'

The age of the informant, therefore, if his lips spoke truth (and the unprecedented dimensions of the body left little doubt on that point), was more than two hundred and thirty-five years. Already he had been the survivor of many important changes in the political and social world around, and would have swum out perhaps as many more had the captors been as solicitous to preserve his life, as they were to take his portrait. This, on the demise of the original, was hung up in the castle of Lautern, and the enormous carcase (which when entire weighed three hundred and fifty pounds, and measured nineteen feet) was sent to the museum of Mannheim, where, deprived of its flesh, and it hung, and haply yet hangs, a light skeleton, which a child might move.

The Angler's Notebook and Naturalist's Record, 1880

Barbel fines

THE BARBEL is not everywhere held so cheap, nor was it always thus despised at home: in Elizabeth's day they were in sufficient repute to be protected by statute law: amongst the piscatory restrictions of her reign, it is enacted that any one taking barbel less than twelve inches shall pay twenty shillings, and give up the fish so wrongfully taken, and the net or engine so wrongfully used; 'and, again, by another enactment,' whoever, fishing in the Severn, makes use of any engine or device, whereby salmon, trout, or barbel be taken, under the several lengths aforesaid, shall pay five shillings, and forfeit the fish and the instruments?

By our Gallic neighbours, who are some authority in these matters, barbel are held in high esteem: at Tours and other inland places situated on rivers, 'Les trois Barbeaux' is a well-known sign; and an abundant supply is always ready for 'noces et festins' [weddings and feasts] in water-cages under the bridge.

We beg, therefore, to assure citizen anglers, and others who may be incredulous, that these fish, simply boiled in salt and water, and eaten cold, with a squeeze of lemon-juice, will be found by no means despicable fare, and we particularly commend to their notice the head and its appurtenances: Bloch recommends to boil them with a bit of bacon to heighten the flavour.

Charles Badham, *Fish Tattle*, 1854

✵

Hook making was valued worldwide at $354 million in 2023.

✵

There are more than sixty different species of flying fish.

✵

The world's rarest fish is the Devils Hole pupfish – a few dozen at most live in one small lake in a cavern in Nevada's Death Valley.

✵

The dwarf sea horse *Hippocampus zosterae* is the slowest swimmer at just 5ft in an hour.

✵

Fastest fish: the sailfish, which inhabits the Pacific and Indian oceans, has been recorded as swimming at just under 70mph.

✵

Angel fish that escape from trawler's nets, remember how they did it and can repeat the trick.

✵

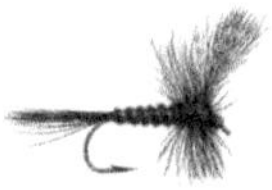

The common carp is so suspicious that it is one of the most difficult fish to catch on rod and line, in the UK at least. In parts of the United States it is considered a pest because it is so easy to catch and so prolific!

Most intelligent

OSCAR FISH have been taught tricks, sea bream learn which humans are likely to feed them and which are not, and manta rays have brain cells comparable with those found in humans.

Very, very small

Photocorynus spiniceps (the spinyhead seadevil) is a weird, spiny tiddler that lives in the Pacific and Indian oceans. Mature males reach a maximum adult size of less than 7mm!

Paedocypris progenetica, the Indonesian superdwarf, is a member of the carp family. It grows to a maximum of 7mm. It was discovered only in 2006. It is almost completely transparent and lives in the swamps of Sumatra and Bintan. It lives in thick brown water which is roughly one hundred times more acidic than rainwater. Even more bizarrely it has no skull – the brain is entirely surrounded by soft tissue.

Deepest

DEEPEST-SWIMMING FISH ever recorded: in 2022 a snailfish was filmed at 8,336m (27,349ft) in the Izu-Ogasawara Trench off the coast of Japan. This broke the previous record of 8,178m set in 2017 by a Mariana snailfish.

Absorbed

ANGLERFISH REPRODUCE when a male attaches itself to the much larger female and gradually fuses with her; the male loses its blood vessels, its eyes and all its internal organs and becomes little more than a fishy skin tag.

Total number

WORLDWIDE THERE are more than 34,000 different species of fish and new species are discovered every year.

The global fishing-rod market was worth more than £962 million in 2024.

In 2019 there were more than 2,000 fishing tackle shops in the UK.

£30,000 fish

THE MOST expensive stuffed fish ever sold fetched more than £30,000 when auctioned in July 2024 – it was our old friend Clarissa, the record carp caught at Redmire Pool by Richard Walker in the early 1950s.

Eating his own weight

THE GROWTH of a pike, under favourable circumstances, during the earlier portion of life, is occasionally at the rate of four pounds per annum; after twelve years he diminishes probably to one or two pounds; and lessens still more as age advances.

When about five years old, he will eat every fortnight his own weight in gudgeons, and do ample justice to his food, by a proportionate increase in size and weight; when old, however, though his appetite may be as good, yet having then many parasites to maintain, the assimilation is not so perfect as in a younger fish.

The Angler's Notebook and Naturalist's Record, 1880

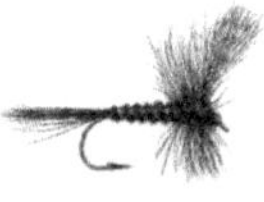

Never allowed to join

GEORGINA BALLANTINE'S famous 64lb salmon from the River Tay was caught in 1922. More than a century later the record still stands. A painting of the fish is proudly displayed in The Flyfishers' Club in London. The irony is that, as a woman, Ballantine was never allowed to join The Flyfishers' Club.

Georgina's record salmon was caught on a spinner and just two years after it was landed, another woman, Clementina 'Tiny' Morrison, landed a 61lb salmon from the River Deveron in Scotland. Ms Morrison's huge fish was caught on a fly – a Brown Wing Killer to be precise.

So, the two biggest salmon ever caught on rod and line in the UK were both landed by women.

Record carp in 1900

THE BIGGEST carp ever landed on rod and line in the UK, up to 1900, was a 23lb 1oz fish caught by George Holden from Broadwater Lake. The current official record is a fish known as The Parrot, caught by Dean Fletcher and weighing 68lb 1oz.

But carp records are strange – for various reasons bigger fish are sometimes not submitted to the record fish committee. A carp known as The Big Plated, weighing 83lb 4oz, was caught in 2017 at Wingham syndicate in Kent for example, but no claim was submitted for it.

Some would say that the 1900 record fish was more impressive than these more recent monsters, which are often caught from lakes where super-large fish have been bred and released; what's more, carp anglers now use long-range hi-tech tackle – including electronic bite alarms – that would have been unavailable a century ago. George Holden's 23lb fish would have been caught on a cane rod, centrepin reel and silk line.

Perhaps there should be a separate modern record category for carp (and other fish) caught without the aid of long-distance reels, nylon lines and electronic gadgetry.

Dabbers for chub

ANOTHER CLASS of Thames fishermen I meet with, are dabbers for chub with cockchafers. These have more retired habits than your punters, and cause themselves to be landed on some ait, or small island in the river, from the banks of which, under the shelter of the willows, with a long rod, a short line, and a lively cockchafer, they often have good sport. The chub is a shy fish, but is readily taken with the bait I have mentioned, if proper caution is used.

Edward Jesse, *An Angler's Rambles*, 1836

Far up the stream

WHO FORGETS his first trout? Mine, thanks to that unlucky star, was a double deception, or rather there were two kinds of deception. A village carpenter very kindly made rods for us. They were of unpainted wood, these first rods; they were in two pieces, with a real brass joint, and there was a ring at the end of the top joint, to which the line was knotted.

We were still in the age of Walton, who clearly knew nothing, except by hearsay, of a reel; he abandons the attempt to describe that machine as used by the salmon-fishers. He thinks it must be seen to be understood.

With these innocent weapons, and with the gardener to bait our hooks, we were taken to the Yarrow, far up the stream, near Ladhope. How well one remembers deserting the gardener, and already appreciating the joys of having no gillie nor attendant, of being 'alone with ourselves and the goddess of fishing'!

I cast away as well as I could, and presently jerked a trout, a tiny one, high up in the air out of the water. But he fell off the hook again, he dropped in with a little splash, and I rushed up to consult my tutor on his unsportsmanlike behaviour, and the disappointing, nay, heartbreaking, occurrence.

Was the trout not morally caught, was there no way of getting him to see this and behave accordingly? The gardener feared there was none. Meanwhile he sat on the bank and angled in a pool. 'Try

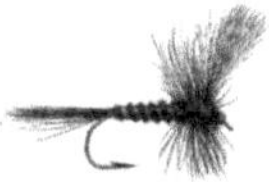

my rod,' he said, and, as soon as I had taken hold of it, 'pull up,' he cried, 'pull up.' I did 'pull up,' and hauled my first troutling on shore.

But in my inmost heart I feared that he was not my trout at all, that the gardener had hooked him before he handed the rod to me. Then we met my younger brother coming to us with quite a great fish, half a pound perhaps, which he had caught in a burn. Then, for the first time, my soul knew the fierce passion of jealousy, the envy of the angler. Almost for the last time, too; for, I know not why it is, and it proves me no true fisherman, I am not discontented by the successes of others. If one cannot catch fish oneself, surely the next best thing is to see other people catch them?

Andrew Lang, *Angling Sketches*, 1891

What Engins?

You see the way the Fisherman doth take
To catch the Fish; what Engins doth he make?
Behold how he ingageth all his wits,
Also his Snares, Lines, Angles, Hooks, and Nets.
Yet fish there be, that neither Hook, nor Line,
Nor Snare, nor Net, nor Engin can make thine;
They must be grop't for, and be tickled too,
Or they will not be catch't, whate'er you do.

John Bunyan, *The Pilgrim's Progress*, 1678

Small fish list

Pandaka pygmaea, the dwarf pygmy goby – just 11mm (0.43in) as a maximum length.

Trimmatom nanus, the midget dwarf goby, which never gets bigger than 10mm (0.39in).

Denise's pygmy sea horse, this measures just 1.35cm (0.5in) long.

Dwarf blowfish, only 22mm (0.8in) long.

Most wonderfully named fish

THE STOUT infantfish (*Schindleria brevipinguis*), which lives off the coast of Australia on the Great Barrier Reef and on the Osprey Reef in the Coral Sea.

Biggest fish in the world

THE WHALE shark reaches 18m (more than 60ft) in length and can weigh more than 20 tonnes. A plankton feeder, it lives across most of the world's tropical oceans, but is threatened as are so many marine species by damaging human activity.

Basking shark – up to 45ft in length and weighing up to 10,000lb. An inhabitant of the world's temperate oceans and a filter feeder.

The great white shark grows to 20ft in length and up to 2,600–3,000lb. It inhabits subtropical and temperate waters.

Giant manta ray – lives in tropical and subtropical seas, has a wingspan of up to around 25ft, and weighs up to 5,500lb.

Tiger shark – tropical and subtropical water, up to 18ft in length.

Heaviest freshwater fish – the beluga sturgeon – specimens are recorded at more than 3,400lb.

The world-record rod-caught brown trout weighed 41.45lb and was caught by Tom Healy in 2009 from the Manistee River system in Michigan, USA.

A 31lb 12oz wild brown trout caught from Loch Awe by Brian Rutland holds the British record.

The wels catfish record stands at 280lb caught from the river Po in Italy in 2015 and released back into the river.

The heaviest of all bony fish is the mola or ocean sunfish, which can weigh more than 5,000lb. Perhaps the oddest looking of all the giant fish, the mola looks like a huge, flattened football.

Sharks, which take the top spots for size and weight, don't have bones; instead their skeletons are made from cartilage. So, although fish, they are members of a different class from bony fish. Chondrichthyes are cartilaginous fish, while bony fish are classified as Osteichthyes.

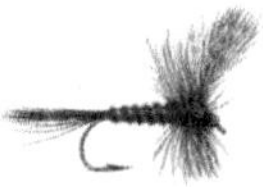

Prized teeth

SHARKS' TEETH have been used for everything from arrow heads to clubs and daggers. Especially prized are teeth like those of the great white shark, that have serrated edges. Some species of shark will grow and regrow as many as 30,000 teeth in a lifetime.

Actually a char

THE SO-CALLED Dolly Varden or bull trout, which lives in North American and Asian streams that run into the Pacific, is actually a char. It gets its name (allegedly) from a character in Charles Dickens' novel, *Barnaby Rudge*. Pollution and habitat destruction have greatly reduced the fish's numbers and it is now listed as 'vulnerable' to extinction.

Total catch

THE TOTAL declared salmon catch in England and Wales was 5,399 fish in 2023, down from 6,952 in 2022. Additionally, the total declared sea trout catch by rod in England and Wales was 11,125 in 2023, a decrease from 12,533 in 2021.

Chalk stream rarity

SOME 85 per cent of the world's chalk streams are found in the UK, and most are in southern and South West England. Chalk stream fishing is seen as the finest in the world but access, given the rarity of chalk streams, is inevitably both limited and very expensive.

Red and gold

AND HERE at last were the rudd, swimming lazily about in the sunshine close to the island, and looking like reddish-brown shadows.

A better point of vantage for the angler could not have been designed. From behind the reeds, I could cast a fly into the middle of the shoal and run no risk of detection if I kept fairly still, and I could also watch its effect.

The fly fell within a foot of the island at the first cast, and was drawn gently away from it. Immediately three fish turned and followed it in a leisurely manner. Presently the line tightened, there was a gentle strike, and a gleam of deep gold showed that rudd No. I was hooked. He was played rather gently at first, so that he might not splash about on the surface and alarm his fellows, but as he was gradually enticed away from the island more pressure was applied, and before long the net was dipped into the water on the other side of the barrier, and his capture was assured.

The fish was a really gorgeous spectacle in the bright sunshine, his scales glowing with a deep red-gold, and his fins as red as blood. He had fought, too, up to every ounce of the pound he weighed.

Then the shoal was attacked again, and a second fish of similar size was hooked and netted in the same manner.

Then came a beauty of one and three-quarter pounds, which proved to be the largest of the day. He was followed by a brace weighing one and a quarter pounds and one and a half pounds respectively, and then the shoal disappeared. There was no fuss, and apparently no panic; it simply vanished, probably into the reeds.

H. T. Sheringham, *An Open Creel*, 1910

Presidential

The gods do not deduct from man's allotted span the hours spent fishing.

Herbert Hoover (1874–1964),
31st United States President

American presidents Dwight Eisenhower, George H. W. Bush, and Theodore Roosevelt all enjoyed fishing.

Mrs Nicholl embraces a salmon

I WENT round and there he was with old Harry Pritchard. He brought out his telescope and we had a look at Crichton and Mrs Nicholl both wading in the river and fishing under the red cliff! I crossed the ditch, climbed the bank and went along the beautiful cliff walk on the edge of the cliff looking over the edge at Mrs Nicholl standing on a rock fishing far below till I came to a steep path leading down the rocks to where Crichton was fishing.

'Henry,' called Mrs Nicholl's voice faintly down the river. 'She has got a good fish,' said Crichton, winding up his line after looking at her a moment.

We scrambled over the rocks to her, but she had landed her fish before we reached her. I was amazed to see Mrs Nicholl coolly wading more than ankle deep in the river with her ordinary lady's boots on. She walked about in the river as if she were on dry land, jumped from rock to rock, slipped off the rocks into the river, scrambled out again, splashed about like a fish. March water is cold. Mrs Nicholl must be an uncommonly plucky woman. Crichton says she rides to hounds and nothing stops her. She does not care what she does.

He hooked a salmon the other day and his boy was clumsy in landing the fish, so Mrs Nicholl plunged into the water on the edge of a deep hole, embraced the great fish round the body, and carried him out in her arms.

Kilvert's Diary, 29 March 1871

Sturgeon in danger

THERE ARE some twenty-eight species of sturgeon, many of which are critically endangered. At least two species are now thought to be extinct. These ancient fish – first found in the fossil record more than 120 million years ago – are long-lived and late to mature. Overfishing and pollution are the main threats, but worse is the building of dams which cuts the fish off from their spawning grounds.

Superficially similar to sharks with smooth skin, sturgeons have a series of armoured plates, known as scutes, running along the lateral line.

Sturgeon were once found across the world from subtropical through temperate to Arctic rivers. A beluga sturgeon caught in Russia in 1827 was more than 23ft long and weighed in excess of 3,400lb.

Wise advice

Fishing is not about patience; it's about controlled impatience.

Richard Walker

Mysterious depths

IN THE heat of noonday I have cruised in a punt upon the surface of that small fathomless pool and looked down among waving weed cables at broad netted backs stirring there in those mysterious depths.

Chris Yates, *The Deepening Pool*, 1990

Biggest ever salmon (not on rod and line)

THE BIGGEST Atlantic salmon ever recorded was netted off the coast of Scotland in 1960. It weighed 109lb (49.44kg). The longest Atlantic salmon ever came from Norway in 1925. It measured 63.25in (160.65cm) from snout to tail.

Oldest hook

THE WORLD'S oldest fish hook comes from East Timor. Unearthed at the Jarimalai cave shelter along with thousands of fish

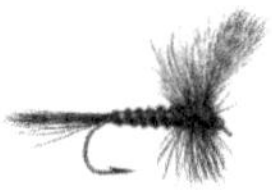

bones the hooks – beautifully fashioned from shells – are somewhere between 16,000 and 23,000 years old.

Earliest reel

THE IDEA of a fishing reel to store line and pay out line when a fish runs, certainly dates back to at least the twelfth century.

An illustration from the Chinese painter Ma Yuan's Southern Song (made in 1195) shows a reel that looks very much like a modern centrepin reel. An earlier but less clear illustration of a reel comes from a decorated stone made during the Han Dynasty (25–220 CE). Multipliers and fixed spool reels are far more recent inventions – both created in the nineteenth century.

Biggest ever

THE BIGGEST fish ever caught on rod and line was a 3,427lb great white shark. Two anglers took the credit for the catch – Frank Mundus and Donnie Braddick. The year was 1986 and the pair were fishing off the coast of Montauk, New York.

Very small records

THE UK British Record Rod-Caught Fish Committee accepts record claims for some very small species. The record gudgeon weighed just under 5oz, the record ruffe a little over 5oz, and the record minnow less than 1oz!

Other tiny records

Bitterling – 12 drams
Bleak – 4oz 9 drams
Bullhead – 1oz
Stickleback – 8g

What makes a rod?

ONLY A few thousand cane rods are now made each year in the UK. The most common rod-making material is carbon fibre (as of 2025) but fibreglass rods are still made and composite rods mixing various materials. Older and once very popular rod-making materials include greenheart and Spanish reed.

Greenheart, or spearwood, comes from South America. This dense timber was wonderfully flexible so perfect for fly fishing. But it had a major fault – a tendency to explode without warning when the angler was playing a fish, i.e. the rod was under strain.

Most expensive reel

THE MOST expensive reel ever sold was a Hotspur Cascapedia Salmon Reel, serial number 001. It went for a staggering £55,000 and was sold in 2017 in aid of the Atlantic Salmon Trust.

Artificial flies with silly names

- Dog Nobbler
- Woolly Bugger
- Chubby Chernobyl
- Hairy Mary
- Adams Parachute
- Batman Nymph
- Bead Head Crystal Bugger

The Coachman, one of the most enduringly popular trout flies ever created, was invented by Queen Victoria's coachman Tom Bosworth.

Roof teeth

TROUT HAVE upper and lower jaws but only the lower jaw moves. They have two rows of vomerine teeth located in the roof of the mouth.

How silk fly lines were made

RAW SILK skeins were washed to remove the sericin, a natural gum. Next came the dyeing. Then the silk was wound onto bobbins. Next came braiding where tapers were made by braiding the silk threads, creating a thicker or thinner line depending on the desired taper.

Loose ends were then trimmed and burnt to create a smooth finish before the line was vacuum impregnated with a traditional varnish, typically linseed oil and natural resins, in multiple coats.

Next came polishing to create a smooth surface. Loops were added to the end of the line to attach the leader.

The one great disadvantage of silk fly lines was that they were expensive – and rotted quickly if not dried at the end of a fishing day.

Trout on a cockroach

ONCE UPON a time when I was a boy I peeped down between waterwheel and floorboards in a disused Kennet mill. Within a few feet of my face appeared a five-pound trout. After long counsel with my father (who at the age of three had drawn barbs on his pot-hooks and landed his first trout) I procured several cockroaches, and, having let my brother into the plot, proceeded in his company to the mill. We did not wear rubber shoes and tread delicately over the old flooring: our plans were better laid than that. We approached the wheel carelessly, sat down and proceeded to discuss general topics.

You see, our idea was to make the trout imagine that the mill was inhabited, and that its inhabitants boded no ill. Possibly our voices were a little strained; but that, of course, the trout would not notice. After a time – it seemed about half an hour – but was probably five minutes, we looked cautiously through a slit in the boards.

There he was! He must have heard us coming, and he had not been alarmed. I released a cockroach from the tin (it was not very easy, for my hands were not as steady as usual), and before the insect had time to find his legs my brother neatly flicked him over the edge.

Our eyes were at the crack even before cocky touched the water, and then – shades of Walton, what a sight! There was a swirl, a broad flash of silver, a sort of 'pop', and when the ripples had subsided, there was the trout and there wasn't the cockroach. This procedure was repeated on the next day and the day following, each time with the same result.

On the fourth day the proceedings were somewhat more involved. The released cockroach had to be caught and transfixed by a No. 5 hook, which was attached to an engine of curious design. My heart goes out to myself in sympathy even now when I think of the palpitations I endured. However, at long last cockroach No. 4 was despatched on his downward career. He reached the water – not so readily nor so steadily as his predecessors it is true; still, he reached the water with quite a goodly plop, and it speaks volumes for my self-control when I say that I refrained from flicking him up high into the air. For the trout rose as usual with that glorious swirl, his nose almost touched the bait, and he stopped dead. Then I saw his pectoral fins backing water. I could swear he glanced up at the chink in the boards, and slowly he retreated a foot.

Then suddenly he turned tail and bolted. I am ashamed to say that I rose up in my wrath and hurled the tin after him; the lid came off and a fleet of cockroaches swam the tide. But so far as I know they all reached the bank in safety.

So far from proving any sagacity in the trout I am certain that this incident proves just the opposite.

The trout undoubtedly saw us the first day, it heard our movements the second and third, and its instinct must have warned it that we were enemies. Why then did it not forsake its abode until the danger was past – as any other sensible animal would have done? Why, it even ate a strange food when within a few yards of a human being. And had not its natural instinct warned it that the fourth cockroach was part of an engine, it would have rushed gladly to its destruction.

Mr Nicoll, whose interesting paper I have already quoted, tells of an attempt to hook a large trout that came to a bridge to be fed with bread every day.

'I never knew him to make the slightest mistake ... However carefully the bread with a hook was thrown in there was doubtless always a little drag, and this was sufficient to put him on his guard, for, however freely he was feeding, the hooked piece was invariably sniffed at and refused.'

The fact of the matter is that the trout is endowed, like most other wild animals, with an instinct which bids it beware not only of humans but of 'engines'. Bait a rat-trap, a gin, never so enticingly but leave the jaws exposed, and you will not catch rats, though the rats may never have seen a gin before.

P. B. M Allan, *Trout Heresy*, 1936

Pike versus stickleback

BY OLD Pikes, Sticklebacks are held in yet greater abomination than Perch, and not without good reason, seeing the havoc they commit amongst the young and unwary Pickerels.

It is only by personal suffering that fish, any more than men, ever buy wisdom; growing Pikes no sooner begin to feel the cravings of hunger, and to find they have large mouths, well furnished with teeth on purpose to cater for it, than they proceed to make preliminary essay upon the smallest fish within reach; these are commonly the Ganterite, or Sticklebacks, who, observing the gaping foe advance against them, prepare for the encounter by bristling up their spines in instinctive readiness to stick in his throat, instead, as he supposes, of going smoothly down into his stomach. This induces a dreadful choking disease, which we venture to call 'stickle-backbites', by means whereof many a promising young Jack pike is cut off in *cuniculis* (in the cradle).

Charles Badham, *Fish Tattle*, 1854

Chicken feed

THE ROUGH-TAILED Stickleback is very generally distributed throughout most parts of England, Ireland, and Scotland, inhabiting indifferently fresh and salt, running and stagnant waters; and, although maturing but few eggs, the numbers of individuals are so great as, according to Pennant, to have enabled a Lincolnshire labourer to earn four shillings a day during a considerable period by catching and selling them at the rate of a halfpenny a bushel – the fish in this case being used as manure.

They are also used for the same purpose near the River Walland, in which, about once in eight years, they are caught by the cartload. Mr Salter assures us that both Sticklebacks and Sprats make excellent food for poultry, which are very fond of them, and fatten amazingly.

Francis Ward, *Marvels of Fish Life*, 1911

Eight hundred gudgeon in three weeks

THE CAPACITY of the Pike for food is well-nigh inexhaustible, and is in analogy with its powers of digestion, the marvellous rapidity of which has been aptly described as resembling the action of fire.

To procure positive data, however, upon this point must clearly be a matter of great difficulty. From frequent opportunities of witnessing the feeding and management of Pike in stews [ponds], I should say that a fish of 5 or 6lb would eat, if permitted, at least twice its own weight of fish every week.

As an instance of this, it is mentioned that eight Pike, of about 5lb each, consumed nearly 800 gudgeons in three weeks, and that the appetite of one of them was almost insatiable. There is no doubt, however, that this dietary is far below the limit which might be reached. In some lochs in Scotland the fish has been known to eat its own weight of baits every day.

Thomas Stoddart, *Angler's Companion*, 1892

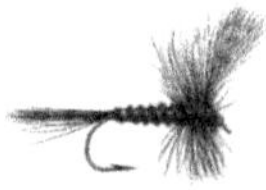

Chapter 10

HOOK, LINE AND SINKER

Why spade end and not eyed hooks?

SPADE END hooks work better than eyed hooks when you are using light lines and very small hooks. Why? Because the flat, spade-shaped end of the hook shank allows the fishing line to be tied in a straight-line connection that reduces the number of bites missed. There is no hinge effect as there often is with an eyed hood which can move out of a straight line. With heavier lines and larger hooks there is little or no discernible difference.

First electronic bite alarm

THE FIRST electronic bite alarm was the Optonic introduced in the early 1980s. It was made by a company called Delkim. An earlier bite alarm, the Heron, was designed by Richard Walker's friend Maurice Ingham in the late 1940s. Walker famously held the British record for carp from the early 1950s until his 44lb fish was beaten by a 51lb 6oz fish caught by Chris Yates in the early 1980s. Both record fish were caught from Redmire Pool and both using cane rods.

Jeers!

THE FOLLOWERS of old Izaak Walton are thought by many to be insignificant characters, and they are subject to all sorts of jeers and insulting remarks.

John Baddeley, *The London Angler's Book or Waltonian Chronicle*, 1834

Benson and Hedges

ONCE VOTED the nation's favourite fish, Benson was the biggest carp ever caught in Northamptonshire as of 2025. She weighed 64lb 6oz. Her sister was known as Hedges. Both fish lived in Bluebell Lakes.

Benson was caught more than sixty times in the space of a dozen or so years. She died in 2009 at around fifteen years of age.

Epigrammatic eel

THE RECOGNISED difficulty of retaining an eel in the hand, has been the subject of several epigrams, both ancient and modern. A Latin one by Gesner, in which he compares man's abortive attempt to hold it, to his equally insecure tenure of life, is not by any means the worst:

How mobile, fleet, and uncontroll'd,
Glides life's uncertain day!
Who clings to it, but grasps an eel,
That quicker slips away.

Fiddling at the fly

THERE WAS only a middling evening rise on any of the days, and the fish did not take madly then; there was a deal of fiddling at the fly, and very little taking.

The last day of the week, Saturday, was a most disappointing day. The wind got round to the north-east, and you could not fish the

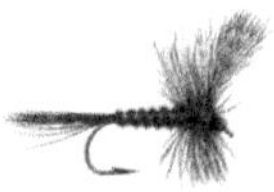

Wood Shallow at all. I tried it once or twice, but found that, between having my line blown back into the trees and hung up or doubled back down stream, it was impossible, and below, the water was threshed to extinction.

I hooked one good fish, but he got off just as he was coming in to the net; after this I rose no end of fish, but not one would fasten. Fish of two and three pounds and larger came at the fly – like bulldogs. The whoosh they made was at times astonishing, but on no occasion did they take the steel. Over and over again, did they pull the fly under water and yet avoid the hook. How they do that I cannot understand and I should hardly credit it if I had not seen it.

Once I saw a fine fish come at the fly with his upper jaw above the water and still he did not take the fly in his mouth. I got quite sick of it at last. Put the fly neatly and fairly over the fish and you might bet two to one you would rise him, and ten to one he wouldn't take.

I must have risen fifty fish from first to last, not one of which took the fly or meant it. What did they come for? There was no evening rise at all so I went home blank and disgusted.

Francis Francis, *Reminiscences*, 1887

The barbel cure

ONE PRECAUTION however should be taken before cooking a barbel; the roe must be entirely removed, as a very small fragment will produce serious internal derangement.

One Antoninus Gazius, undertook, as a warning to mankind, to eat two mouthfuls of barbel roe, and not more than as many hours after the experiment, was attacked with symptoms as alarming as those produced by Asiatic cholera – racking pains and purging, cold extremities, and delirium; and in the second stage of his illness he experienced such a prolonged state of vital prostration that his friends fairly gave him up: yet in spite of these recitals, this pernicious roe … was at no remote period mercilessly used as a remedy in medicine.

Charles Badham, *Fish Tattle*, 1854

Chub-faced fop

AMONGST THE white freshwater fish included under this heading are many species of which we would fain speak: the L. *rutilus* (roach), whose frisky movements have caused him to be considered as the fit emblem of robust health, and thus made the proverb 'sound as a roach' familiar to the ear as the form of the well-known subject of it is to the eye; the L. *cephalus* (chub), whose obese body, empty head, and inflated face, helped the Stratford bard (who must often have pulled them out of the Avon) to the simile:

> I never saw a fool lean; the chub-faced fop shines sleek
> with full-cramm'd fat of happiness.

The L. *vulgaris* (dace), comes in for a share of Walton's gentle wish:

> Let me live harmlessly, and near the brink
> Of Trent or Avon have a dwelling-place,
> Where I may see my quill or cork down sink,
> With eager bite of perch, or bleak, or dace.

Several of these small and apparently insignificant fish are borne, notwithstanding their diminutive size, as heraldic badges of distinction. The family De la Roche (whose first progenitor, Adam De la Roche, founded, as far back as about the year 1200, Roche Castle and a Benedictine priory in Pembrokeshire, and gave rise to a wide-spreading posterity) is proud to bear [in its coat of arms] three roach naiant (i.e. swimming horizontally). The Pictons adopt three minnows or pentis. While ... three chub, sable, arc the arms of the Chubb family, and borne by Lord Dormer of Wenge, on one of his quarterings.

Moule gives a much more probable explanation of the phrase, which he derives from the legend of St Roche, who was fabled to cure, on proper importunity, those afflicted with any grievous plague, restoring them to perfect health. 'Sound as a roche,' then, seems to be a metonymy for 'sound as one of St Roche's patients'.

Charles Badham, *Fish Tattle*, 1854

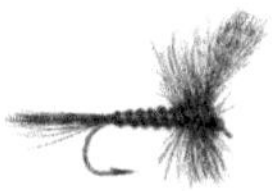

Fishy jewellery

THE PEARLY matter here is not procured, as in the bleak, from the washing of the scales, but from the swim-bladder itself, which, previous to trituration [breaking down into powder], looks like some fine orient pearl lying in the body of the fish, an appearance rendered more striking from the strong contrasts it presents to the stomach, which is quite black.

No sooner are these soft silvery bladders extracted, than they are instantly plunged into a bottle of spirits-of-wine, which preserves their beauty unimpaired till the artificer has occasion to use them; he then macerates the requisite number in a solution of isinglass till all the pearly particles are detached; and having already prepared a supply of filmy glass beads of different shapes, he introduces, by means of a blowpipe, a layer of the pearl liquid into the interior of each through a small hole left for the purpose at both ends of the bead.

The better to distribute it equally throughout the cavity he gently shakes them on a sieve, and after repeating the operation once or twice till all look solid, fills up any remaining vacancy with fused wax, clears out the orifices of the holes to remove any obstruction, and finally strings them upon strong silk thread, ready for sale.

Amongst the many false things sold in the city of Rome for genuine valuables, these counterfeits, which are never intended to deceive purchasers, are by far the most graceful. Mixed up with much vile modern bronze, flaunting shell cameos, pigmy temples in giallo or mosaic trash, and all the false coinage and pseudo-antique gems palmed off on foreign public for genuine, Argentine pearls always look well, and but for their low price would be universally admired. The whole gear of necklace, bracelets, brooch, and earrings may be bought for a few scudi.

The Angler's Notebook and Naturalist's Record, 1880

Fashionable angler

WHENEVER I see a gentleman dressed in fashionable angling costume – broad-brimmed straw hat, new short-lapped coat, caoutchouc [natural rubber] boots and a dirty looking broad-striped shirt – angling with an 18ft rod in a stream he might stride over, I set him down as a novice …

Stephen Oliver, *Scenes and Recollections of Fly Fishing*, 1834

Bull trout

WRITERS INCLUDING H. T. Sheringham, insist bull trout are found in the River Coquet, but they were never there. *Salmo eriox* is no longer seen as a separate species, just a type of large brown trout found in North East England and South East Scotland.

First nylon line

THE AMERICAN company DuPont was the first to manufacture nylon fishing line, thus beginning the gradual (but still not quite complete!) extinction of silk and gut lines. The first nylon line appeared in 1939 but it was stiff and difficult to use. It took another twenty years for a more supple line to appear – this was DuPont Stren.

Earliest waders

THE EARLIEST fishing waders were manufactured by the Hodgman Company in the 1830s using oil-impregnated canvas. Rubber began to be used around 1912 and improved greatly over the following years. By 2025 natural rubber had been superseded by synthetic rubber (neoprene).

Sturgeon from Cornwall

FISHING A lake in Cornwall in 1991, Tony Chater landed a bizarre-looking fish that no one seemed able to identify. It had huge, glowing eyes, an almost otherworldly appearance, and skin that seemed to shimmer in the moonlight. The first reports suggested it was possibly an alien species or some kind of genetic mutation. Eventually, scientists identified it as a species of sturgeon, but at the time the catch sparked wild rumours about UFOs and extraterrestrial life.

Salmon forfeit

AMONG THE regulations to protect the salmon the party who catch and send salmon to London for sale the produce of any fishery of less than six pounds weight, forfeits five pounds; the said penalty applies to the buyer and seller of the fish.

Nineteenth-century ordinance

Choosing your tackle a century ago

THE FIRST item of discussion will be the rod, and the novice will be invited to inspect a stiff general rod, made up of two or three cane joints and a greenheart top. Its length will be about 12ft, its weight about 15oz, and its cost may be anything from ten shillings to forty.

I have an excellent old rod of this nature for which years ago I gave 6s.6d.; it still sees service, and is Jack of all trades. For a guinea the novice ought to get a weapon which will do all that is required at first.

He should try the rod in his hand, with a reel attached to its butt, and so make sure that it feels comfortable, and he should not accept a rod if it feels at all top-heavy and ill-balanced, if the weight greatly exceeds 16oz for 12ft, or if the grip of the butt does not suit his hand.

Reels

The reel or winch, is the next object which the novice must acquire, and it is probable that he cannot do better than purchase the wooden Nottingham reel, with which the rod was balanced, if its price is not prohibitive. I recommend a good reel, for in some ways the angler is more dependent on it than on his rod; an inferior article, which warps after the least exposure to damp or whose machinery comes to grief at the least extra strain, is a fearful possession.

I have three or four ancient Nottingham reels, relics of the past, which refuse to turn round at all, and they are a perpetual sermon about the follies of penny wisdom. But I acquired them in days when good reels were not so plentiful as they are now. Besides being good the novice's reel should I think, be rather large; four inches are not too many for its diameter, in my opinion, though many anglers are content with something smaller.

Lines

The third requirement is the line to be put on the reel. In this matter, too, there is ample scope for choice (and for confusion); but, on the whole it is best for the novice to aim at simplicity.

This, I think, he is most likely to achieve with a fine waterproofed or 'dressed' silk line, of the size marked F or G in the tackle catalogues. Fifty yards of such a line need not cost more than about 5s, but the best quality would be about twice as much.

In selecting it, attention should be paid to its appearance and texture; green is a good colour, though colour does not very much matter, and the texture should be smooth, solid, and pliant; a sticky line is usually an ill-dressed one, and a line that is too stiff and hard is one which has been dried too quickly; both kinds should be avoided. The tackle maker may suggest an undressed line, but at first the novice should have none of it.

Split shot

The novice now has both tackle and bait, and is ready to go fishing; but it is just as well for him to make up his gut lines before he does so, as that is a thing which is most comfortably done at home.

In its dry state gut is rather brittle and apt to crack, therefore he begins by putting four of his casts (one thick, two medium, and one fine) and four hooks (two large and two small) into lukewarm water, so that they may soak. After ten minutes he takes out one of the medium casts and a large hook, unwinds the one and attaches the other to it by joining the two loops thus: the cast loop is passed through the hook loop and then the hook is passed through the cast loop and the two lengths of gut are pulled tight. Next one of the split shots is pinched on to the cast just above the loop, about 18in from the hook (I always perform the pinching with my teeth, and have been sternly rebuked for it more than once. Tiny pairs of pliers are sold as a corrective to this habit).

More on shot

Traditionally, shot (small lead pellets) were made by pouring molten lead through a screen into water, a process that created round pellets known as swan shot. This method was later improved by using a shot tower, a tall structure where the lead droplets could cool and solidify into spherical shapes before hitting the ground or water. Modern manufacturing often uses the Bliemeister method which agitates molten lead passing through screens to achieve the same spherical shape without the need for a shot tower.

Worms

One or two more things remain to be done as a conclusion to the first day's fishing after the novice gets home. The worms, for instance, if any quantity of the original stock remain, are worth preserving against another occasion, and they should be taken out of their bag or tin and put into a tub or box of earth. Otherwise, they may be forgotten and only recalled to mind when they have become a public nuisance. This is, if possible, to be avoided.

In most domestic circles an angler is viewed with something akin to suspicion, as a person who disturbs the even tenor of household ways. Dead worms might undoubtedly tend to give colour to accusations founded on this suspicion.

Line drying

Another thing to be attended to is the drying of the line, or so much of it as has been in the water. The back of a chair can be used for this purpose, and the novice should coil the line on it by walking round and round the chair, reel in hand, and so pulling the line off; the line should not be pulled off with the hand and then coiled round the chair, because this, after a time or two of drying, tends to put a kink or a twist in it, which may ultimately become a nuisance.

The line can be wound back on to the reel by a reverse movement next morning. Better than a chair back is a line dryer, a square frame of light metal or wood which is turned on an axle by means of a handle; fastened by its own little vice to the corner of a table, it winds the line straight off the reel without any risk of kinking. I find my line dryer (which cost about four shillings) extremely useful when I want to change a line from one reel to another, or to take it off for any purpose. The novice, however, has no such need at present.

Eric Parker et al., *Fine Angling for Coarse Fish*, 1921

The smelt is known in Germany as the *stink fisck*.

The old word for grayling is 'umber'. Only very big umber were known as grayling.

Skull on the line

IN 1906, a Thames angler landed a human skull. Its features were badly worn suggesting it had been in the water for a long time. A police investigation began, but no one ever found out exactly where the skull came from or how it ended up in the river. Without modern DNA and other tests, it was impossible to say just how old the skull really was. It could have been ancient or, more gruesomely, it could have been a skull belonging to a recent murder victim.

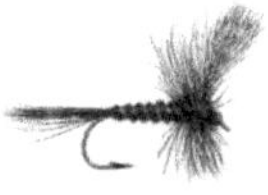

Biggest grayling

THE LARGEST grayling in the kingdom are found in the Itchen and Test, where I have caught them up to 41b weight, and, though a three-pounder is not caught every day, 21b fish are common. They have increased greatly of late years, and some of these waters now abound with them.

Francis Francis, *A Book on Angling*, 1867

Salmon letter

IN 2007, an American angler caught a salmon with a strange, crumpled-up note inside. The note was written in Russian, but was largely indecipherable with only one or two words – such as 'happy holiday' – still clear. The discovery sparked a frenzy of newspaper articles about salmon being used to carry messages for Russian spies – no one seems to have considered the difficulty of persuading the salmon when, where, and how to deliver their messages!

Tramping to the river

UPON THE merits and delights of angling I need scarcely descant. Every angler knows that his feet are never put to the ground with such alacrity and right goodwill, as when tramping to the river, rod in hand, full of hope and expectation, on a fine April morning.

Serenely happy, he then proclaims a universal amnesty to every created being (except an opposition angler), and feeling internally at peace with himself, the world, and all mankind, every object that meets his view seems to wear the same sunny smile that gilds his own happy reflections.

Would that all our dealings and pursuits in the ordinary avocations of daily life were productive of such blessed results!

The Angler's Notebook and Naturalist's Record, 1880

Twenty-pound salmon from the Thames

HAVING GIVEN this account of what I consider to be the inferior kind of fishing in the river Thames, I will now, loving reader, say somewhat respecting the trout fishers.

These are generally first-rate performers, and proofs of their skill may frequently be found by markings or outlines of fish on the walls, or preserved by paintings, at some of the comfortable little inns near the banks of the Thames, between Ditton and Windsor, and probably much higher up.

Thus, June 25, 1918, Mr D'Almaine caught, at Hampton Deep, two trout, one weighing eight pounds and a half, and the other seven pounds.

Perhaps, however, the greatest feat which has been thus commemorated, is the following:

October 30, 1812, at Shepperton Deeps, Mr G. Marshall, of Brewer Street, London, caught a salmon with single-gut, without a landing net, weighing twenty-one and a quarter pounds. The picture of this salmon has, I believe, been lately removed from Shepperton to Staines.

Edward Jesse, *An Angler's Rambles*, 1836

No flies for tench

TENCH ARE no fly-takers; and fishing on the floor is the way to get them. Hooked, tench belie their leisurely habits, fight like demons, and keeping them out of the weeds and bringing them to net is the deuce of a job.

Faddist, *Memorable Coarse Fish*, 1953

Artificial carp?

A 105lb (47.5kg) common carp was caught from the Euro Aqua carp farm in Hungary in 2025 by British angler David Knock. Fishing in a carp farm may seem rather artificial to some but

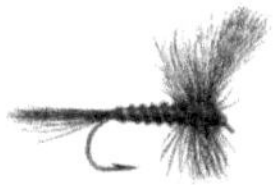

the carp farm lake has produced numerous 90lb-plus fish. Many anglers would perhaps prefer to fish for wild carp a tenth of the size.

Love of fishing

I KNOW no sort of men less subject to melancholy than anglers; many have cast off other recreations and embraced it, but I never knew any angler wholly cast off, though occasions might interrupt, their affections to their beloved recreation; and if this art may prove a *Noble brave rest* to thy mind, it will be satisfaction to his, who is thy well-wishing Friend.

Robert Venables, *The Experienced Angler*, 1662

A kind of madness

ONCE AN angler, always an angler; years roll by only to increase the fervour of our devotion. It is a quiet, simple, unassuming kind of madness, without any of the excitement or the glamour of the race meeting or of the hunting field, and the love and the madness are incomprehensible and inexplicable to those who neither share them nor know them.

H. V. Hart-Davis, *Chats on Angling*, 1906

Gudgeon numbers

MOST ENGLISH rivers and canals produce these fish, occasionally in such numbers, that I have known as many as twelve dozen to be taken at a single throw of the casting-net; and Thompson mentions they were so numerous in the Newforge mill-stream, on the Lagan, Ireland, that the miller's dog at that place was in the habit of catching them with his mouth, and devouring them in quantities.

H. Cholmondeley-Pennell, *The Angler Naturalist*, 1875

Tench in a hole

PITS FROM which brick-clay has been dug often abound with Tench; and a bucketful have been known to be taken out of a hole of this sort not wider than a boy could jump over, and where the weeds were so thick as to be almost solid. In fact, like the Carp, with which they have many habits in common, they appear to prefer foul and weedy to clear waters; and such as produce the one species will very constantly be found to produce the other.

In weight the Tench seldom exceeds 5 or 6lb, although heavier specimens are occasionally caught; the largest on record weighed somewhat over 11lb and was taken from just such a pit as that above described, where it had probably battened for half a century.

A piece of water which had been ordered to be filled up, and into which wood and rubbish had been thrown for years, was directed to be cleared out. Labourers were accordingly employed; and, almost choked up by weeds and mud, so little water remained that no person expected to see any fish, except a few Eels; yet nearly two hundred Tench were netted out.

After the pond was thought to be quite free, under some roots there seemed to be an animal which was conjectured to be an otter: the place was surrounded; and on opening an entrance among the roots a Tench was found of most singular form, having literally assumed the shape of the hole in which he had of course for many years been confined. His length from eye to caudal fork was 33 inches; his circumference, almost to the tail, was 27 inches; his weight 11lb 9½oz: the colour was also singular, his belly being that of a char, or vermilion.

This extraordinary fish, after having been inspected by many gentlemen, was carefully put into a pond, and at the time this account was written, twelve months afterwards, was alive and well.

William Barker Daniel, *Rural Sports*, 1801

Softening the line

ALWAYS MAKE it a rule when angling for roach, chub and barbel to let your line remain with the plummet attached to it, in the water, while you are preparing and casting in groundbait, by which means the line gets stretched and softened and consequently, less likely to break which gut and hair frequently do when dry and stiff.

Thomas Salter, *The Art of Angling*, 1833

Smelts at London Bridge

SMELTS ARE well known as a most delicious Fish for the table. They are of an elegant shape, covered with loose white scales; the back is of a dark hue, but the sides and belly are almost transparent, and shine like silver; the eyes have also the same silvery appearance; their jaws and tongue have many teeth, and very large for so small a fish.

Though they arrive twice every year in the Thames, that is, in March and July, yet, it is said, they do not get above London Bridge during their last visit. When they arrive, if the season is favourable for the Fishermen to work their nets, they then take, or rather used to take, an immense quantity of them, which enabled the poor Fisherman to discharge some of the debts he unavoidably contracts in Winter, in consequence of his not being able to labour in his vocation.

Between London Bridge and Lambeth, is the principal place for taking Smelts in nets; but, for the last twenty years past, those poor Fishermen have been deprived of their resource for paying off the debts of Winter, by the Smelts not making their annual appearance in the river Thames, previous to the time above alluded to. The river used to swarm with this delicious Fish.

In July, we used to begin angling for Smelts, in the various wet docks, below bridge; but at the floating timber, laying at Limehouse hole, was a favourite place for Smelt-fishing; from those timbers a hundred dozen have frequently been taken in a day.

Then, again, Perry's Dock, Blackwall, now belonging to the East India Company, was a place for Smelts in those days!

From this place, it was noways unusual for an expert Angler to carry away upwards of twenty dozen of fine Smelts. I have, very frequently, taken five or six dozen before eight o'clock in the morning, and returned home to breakfast, then residing about two miles from the spot; but this dock, as well as the river, is nearly deserted by the

Smelts; in fact, there has been so few, for several years past, that myself and many others, have entirely declined troubling ourselves about them.

The only place, at present, they are sought after, is in the City Canal, but they are very small in size, and few in number. I have made much inquiry on the subject of the Smelts not visiting, as usual, the river Thames, but without any satisfactory result.

Edward Jesse, *Angler's Rambles*, 1836

Books we should not have forgotten

The Art of Angling, Rock, and Sea-Fishing (1740) by Richard Brookes

An English physician and author, Richard Brookes published multiple works, with *The Art of Angling* being his second. The original edition included 133 woodcut illustrations.

In 1793 Brookes named the first dinosaur from a found bone. Although the bone came from what we call today a Megalosaurus, the original name given to the dinosaur by Brookes was *Scrotum humanum*.

The Young Angler's Pocket Companion (1795) by Ralph Cole

First published in London, this was also known as a *New and Complete Treatise on the Art of Angling, as may be Practised with Success in Every River in England: During Both the Winter and Summer Seasons*. An early guide for young fishermen, it included bait and fly-fishing techniques, and the first edition featured methods for trolling.

The Perfect reel

THE MOST famous fly-fishing reel ever made is the Perfect, manufactured in various incarnations for more than a century by Hardy's of Alnwick in Northumberland.

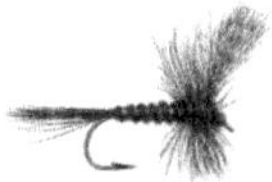

Hardy's was founded in 1872 by brothers William and John Hardy. The company quickly became one of the most successful fishing tackle manufacturers in the world, their name even today a byword for quality.

Their Perfect series of fly-fishing reels launched in 1891 still exists today though it has been updated and modernised over the years. Antique Hardy reels still fetch the highest prices of any fishing tackle at auction.

Famous coarse reel

THE MOST famous coarse fishing reel ever made is probably the Allcock Aerial. Like all centrepin reels, the Aerial is far more difficult to use well than modern fixed spool reels, but for many purists it is the only reel worth using. The reel's distinctive spoked wheel design with circular holes in the rim to reduce weight makes it unmistakable.

Manufactured by the Redditch-based Allcock tackle firm, the Aerial stayed in production from the late 1800s until around 1965. It was made in a variety of styles and sizes but the Match Aerial, its final incarnation, is still eagerly sought by collectors who generally buy it to use.

Allcock, which was founded in 1803, was one of the oldest fishing tackle makers in the world. Sadly, it is no longer in existence.

Orwell's cow-ponds

BUT FISHING was the real thing. We went many a time to old Brewer's pool, and took tiny carp and tench out of it, and once a whopping eel, and there were other cow-ponds that had fish in them and were within walking distance on Saturday afternoons.

But after we got bicycles, we started fishing in the Thames below Burford Weir. It seemed more grown-up than fishing in cow-ponds. There were no farmers chasing you away, and there are thumping fish in the Thames – though, so far as I know, nobody's ever been known to catch one.

George Orwell, *Coming up for Air*, 1939

*

Fishing is a discipline in the equality of men – for all men are equal before fish.

Ernest Hemingway (1899–1961)

*

A bad day of fishing is better than a good day at work.

Ted Hughes (1930–1998)

*

Many men go fishing all of their lives without knowing that it is not fish they are after.

Attributed to Henry David Thoreau

Trout stats

ACCORDING TO the Wild Trout Trust some Icelandic trout reach weights of 10lb and more on a diet consisting almost entirely of small black flies; some 4 to 5 per cent of Tweed juvenile game fish are actually trout-salmon hybrids; brown trout are so genetically variable that it has been suggested they should be split into at least fifty different species; in an extraordinary example of interspecies dependency it appears that freshwater pearl mussels rely on brown trout for a major part of their life cycle; they [the tiny mussels] live in the brown trout's gills (and also in salmon and char gills) before at around one year dropping off and burrowing into the river bed.

Still silk

AS OF 2025 silk lines were still being made in Sheffield. They float better than plastic lines, they cast better (being thinner and denser than

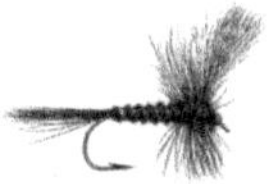

plastic) and they are completely limp so don't retain loops and kinks (i.e. they have no memory facets). Depending on whether they are greased or not they can be used as a floating line or a sinker. There are two drawbacks: they must be looked after carefully or they will rot, and they are expensive. They cost roughly double a good mid-range plastic line.

Pilot jigs

SECOND WORLD War pilots were always issued with a survival kit. It included a small amount of food, a basic medical kit, artificial lures, small jigs and spinners – and fishing line. Presumably, this was in case they crashed and were marooned on an island or were stuck in a forest where a lake or river might give them a chance to catch their dinner.

Duffers' Fortnight

BEFORE POLLUTION and widespread habitat destruction, the mayfly season on England's chalk streams was one of the most exciting times in the angling year. For roughly two weeks the mayfly would hatch and die in enormous numbers leading to a feast for the trout which seemed to lose all caution. The result was that even the most inexperienced angler could catch fish after fish on dry imitations of mayfly – hence the mayfly season was known as Duffers' Fortnight.

Most reprinted

AFTER THE Bible and Shakespeare, the most reprinted book in English in the world is Izaak Walton's *The Compleat Angler* first published in 1653. Remarkably the book isn't really about fishing; it has far more to do with friendship centred on fishing, and nature.

Carp numbers

THE CARP family of fishes – the cyprinids – which includes in the UK roach, chub and carp, is believed to hold the record for the greatest number of species – approximately 1,780 across 166 genera.

One of Izaak Walton's most often quoted remarks is: 'Study to be quiet.'

Greedy

THE BOG trout had a smaller trout halfway down its gullet in a partially digested state which, when it was taken, must have weighed at least two ounces. Even a fish half in its mouth and half in its gullet did not stop the trout from rising at the minnow bait, but its mouth being so full it could not get hold of it, and it was only after repeated rises that it was caught by the outside of the mouth.

P. B. M. Allan, *Trout Heresy*, 1936

Omnivorous

BUT PERHAPS the zenith of the trout's fastidiousness in the matter of food is recorded by a writer in *The Field* (September 23, 1926) who reports finding the following in the stomach of a 3lb 5oz trout, caught on a Coachman, in the Derbyshire Wye between Haddon Hall and Bakewell:

> Worms, snails, half a burnt matchstick, piece of coal, four-inch-long piece of an old paint brush or shaving brush, two inches of a rasher of bacon with the rind on, pieces of onion, celery stalk or hemlock stalks, and what looked like bits of wax candle. The fish was fat and healthy, flesh white, flavour like the mixture of contents.

P. B. M Allan, *Trout Heresy*, 1936

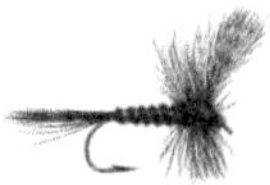

Baby pike

AT EVERY few yards as one walks there is a small boil in the water close to the bank, and if one stops to look one soon sees a baby pike, poised a yard out, and returning one's gaze out of the corner of a watchful eye.

Though he dashed off in such a hurry on being disturbed, he is not really alarmed. Even a tiny pike of four or five inches seems to have hereditary pride of race, to know that his family is the most formidable in the fresh waters, and that he has very little to be afraid of, except, perhaps, an encounter with his own grandparents.

H. T. Sheringham, *An Open Creel*, 1910

Tasty bullhead

WHETHER THE fish is ever captured in this country for edible purposes, I am not aware: M. Risso says that it is eaten in Italy; Mattioli, an eminent physician of the sixteenth century, commends it highly for its 'taste and nourishment;' and Wilson, the naturalist, ascertained that its flesh when boiled becomes red, like that of the salmon.

In Russia the bullhead is used by some as a charm against fever, while others suspend it horizontally, carefully balanced by a single thread; and thus poised, but permitted at the same time freedom of motion, they believe that it possesses the property of acting as a weathercock, and of indicating, by the direction of the head, the point of the compass from which the wind blows.

H. Cholmondeley-Pennell, *The Angler Naturalist*, 1875

Destiny!

THINK OF that lucky fellow who got the 50-pounder and a 35-pounder on the only day he ever went salmon fishing in his life. You wouldn't believe it.

But the men that I have over and over again seen come down just for one day's fishing, and catch big Thames trout that I have fished for months, and all that sort of thing, don't you know, it is positively – well, never mind! It's destiny, that's what it is – kismet, as the Turks say.

Francis Francis, *Reminiscences*, 1887